Creative cost and management accounting

Creative cost and management accounting

Leslie Chadwick MBA, FCCA, Cert.Ed.
Michael Magin BSc.(Econ), MBA, SCMA

Hutchinson Education

An imprint of Century Hutchinson Ltd
62–65 Chandos Place, London WC2N 4NW

Century Hutchinson Australia Pty Ltd
89–91 Albion Street, Surry Hills,
New South Wales 2010, Australia

Century Hutchinson New Zealand Ltd
PO Box 40–086, Glenfield, Auckland 10, New Zealand

Century Hutchinson South Africa (Pty) Ltd
PO Box 337, Bergvlei, 2012 South Africa

First published 1989

Typeset in 11 on 12pt Palatino

Printed and bound in Great Britain by
Butler & Tanner Ltd, Frome and London

British Library Cataloguing in Publication Data

Chadwick, Leslie
    Creative Cost and Management Accounting
    1. Cost Accounting
    I. Title   II. Magin, Michael
    657,42
    ISBN 0 09 173135 6

Contents

Preface

Why Creative Cost and Management Accounting?

The objectives of the book are as follows:

1 To help develop a more critical approach towards cost and management accounting.
2 To expose unsound practices which may exert a significant influence on the decision making process.
3 To create an awareness of the limitations to certain cost and management accounting techniques in those who prepare and those who are the users of the data.
4 To encourage more time and thought to be devoted to the setting of objectives for cost and management accounting methods/systems.
5 To promote the belief that a sophisticated understanding of the nature of cost requires 'creativity' in producing a useful, meaningful, and understandable 'cost'. 'Creative' is used in the sense of 'constructiveness' and 'objectivity' in order to meet a specified objective: namely, the provision of cost information pertinent to the needs of the user.
6 To improve the readers' understanding of cost-information, to the extent that they support the authors' beliefs that:
   (a) there is no such thing as 'the cost' of anything;
   (b) 'cost' is what it is defined to be;
   (c) the definition of cost must follow an understanding of how the cost is to be used; and
   (d) the responsibility for its use is that of the decision-maker, not of the information provider.

For whom is it written?
For qualified accountants; managers; professional accounting students and students on accounting and business studies BEC and degree courses.

Why read it?
We have done our best to adopt a style which is readable, interesting and informative. The chapters include all/some of the following features:

- A critical discussion/evaluation.
- Examples of creativity – short practical examples and mini-cases.
- A brief review of a selected sample of relevant literature.

- The reproduction of relevant articles from leading professional journals.
- A summary at the end of each chapter.

Did you know?
That some companies have been guilty of discontinuing the production of quite profitable products because of the way in which those products were costed!

This is just one of the many examples of creative cost and management accounting which are described within this book.

Acknowledgements

We would like to express our grateful thanks to:

The Administrative Management Society, USA
The Chartered Association of Certified Accountants
The Chartered Institute of Cost and Management Accountants
The Institute of Management Services
Lafferty Publications (*The Accountants Weekly* and *The Accountant*)
The National Association of Accountants, USA (*Management Accounting*, USA)
Newman Publishing Ltd (*Retail and Distribution Management*)
Publishing Horizons, Inc. of Columbus, Ohio, USA
Simon Schuster (Prentice-Hall, Inc.)

for their permission to reproduce certain journal articles and extracts which we feel
make this into a better book.

Part I

An introduction
Costs and cost classification

1

An introduction to creative cost and management accounting

The output generated by the cost and management accounting function in any organization plays a prominent part in the decision making process. In fact, the role of the cost and management accountant has been described quite frequently as that of an information manager. Thus, it is of paramount importance that the information which is provided is accurate, timely and relevant to the purpose for which it is required. In performing their duties the cost and management accounting function must of necessity exercise considerable judgement. Faced with the same problem cost and management accountants working for different firms in the same industry are quite likely to come up with different results. This situation arises because of human nature. Human beings are quite complex variables and may not always act rationally to certain environmental changes. The situation also arises because many of the judgements which have to be made are subjective and may involve a number of qualitative factors, e.g. qualitative objectives, the pre-determination of costs and revenues, the absorption of overheads, etc.

From a behavioural point of view the cost and management function, and in particular the cost and management accountant, can command a considerable influence upon the decision making process. The cost and management accounting function tends to be located at a very important information junction (*see* Fig. 1.1). The function collects, collates and controls the flow of information from within the organization and from outside the organization. The function can regulate and/or restrict the flow of information upwards and downwards as it desires. Whether or not information is transmitted could well depend upon departmental/personal goals and/or perceptions of managerial wishes, policies and objectives. Yes, information may be suppressed! If one could listen in to conversations within the cost and management accounting function, one may overhear statements such as:

'Top management must not get hold of this information or all hell will be let loose!'

'We must ensure that all of the foremen and supervisors are provided with this data and highlight ...'

'Just throw it away, I can't see how it could possibly be of any use to us.'

'This must be re-drafted before it goes to the managing director and that particular part referring to ... must be omitted completely.'

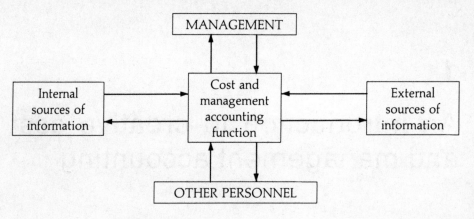

Fig 1.1   The cost and management information junction

Thus, certain information may be destroyed, lost in the files or amended. Behaviouralists would describe the role/position of the cost and management accounting function as being that of 'gate keeper' (Fig. 1.1), i.e. sitting on an important information junction and being able to control the flow of information. This does not mean that the cost and management accounting function will abuse its important position but it could do if it so wished! Many of the decisions which need to be made re the flow of information will be based upon subjective judgement.

The standing of the function may be such that certain personnel, e.g. the cost and management accountant, may have 'political access'. Political access is rather like the situation in history, where a particular individual, e.g. a baron or chief had 'the King's ear'. Thus, political access in an organization occurs where certain individuals are in a position where they can influence the decision takers, e.g. direct access to the managing director. This means that such individuals have even greater power at being creative! Other behavioural factors that may affect creativity are empire building, the quest for power and departmental rivalry.

The word 'cost' is such a widely used word, both by the public at large and the business person, that its meaning is often taken for granted. The authors have found from their lengthy experiences of business and local government, often as the providers of 'cost information', that the word 'cost' is frequently considered an absolute. Even sophisticated business people demonstrate a naivety in asking for 'the cost' of something, or for doing something. Responsibility for producing 'the cost' is often given to the management (or cost) accountant, who often unwittingly perpetuates the myth of 'the cost' by producing one on demand!

Claret (1987) has said that, 'A large part of the management accounting role is educational.' This book was born out of a desire to educate accountants, management and students of business studies and accountancy that:

1 There is no such thing as 'the cost' of anything,
2 'Cost' is what it is defined to be,
3 The definition of cost must follow an understanding of:
   (a) how the cost is to be used, and

(b) the responsibility for its use is that of the decision-maker, not of the information provider.

This book will be biased towards manufacturing industry, although many of the points raised will be relevant to other areas such as services and the public sector. The principal objectives which we hope to achieve are as follows:

1   To encourage the development of a more critical approach to cost and management accounting. This, it is hoped should put a stop to the practice of simply applying cost and management accounting techniques without any thought as to their relevance and limitations.
2   To expose some of the unsound practices which may exert a significant influence upon the decision making process. Thus, making a contribution towards better decision making and the quest for more relevant costing data.
3   To create a greater awareness of the limitations of cost and management accounting techniques and the data which they generate. This, it must be stressed is aimed at both those who provide the information/data and those who are to use/interpret it (e.g. management).
4   To encourage more time and thought to be devoted to the setting of objectives for cost and management accounting systems and techniques. This should possibly help to dictate when, where, why and how such systems and techniques are to be used.
5   To provide a structure against which management can both specify the 'costs' which they require, and/or evaluate the 'costs' provided to them.
6   To promote the quest for more sophisticated systems and techniques e.g. techniques that do recognize the existence of numerous variables which can be applied to the real world of business.

An in-depth understanding of the nature of cost often requires some 'creativity' in producing a useful, meaningful and understandable 'cost'. The provision of cost-data should not just be seen as a routine task, although certain aspects of its preparation can be produced in a systematic way. This is not to say that this book should support the *Creative Accounting* described by Griffiths (1986) who claimed that:

• The use of creative accounting by companies to manipulate the figures reported in their annual accounts is widespread, and that
• Companies produce figures which are only loosely based on fact.

Creative cost and management accounting could support creative accounting either deliberately or unwittingly, although the Statement of Ethical Conduct for Management Accountants produced by the National Association of Accountants (USA) (this is reproduced in full as Appendix A) requires that management accountants have a responsibility, *inter alia*, to:

• Perform their professional duties in accordance with relevant laws, regulations and technical standards.
• Disclose fully all relevant information that could reasonably be expected to influence an intended user's understanding of the reports, comments and recommendations presented.

Similarly, the Chartered Institute of Management Accountants (in the UK) has issued in its Statement on standards of professional conduct and competence (ICMA, July 1986) standards on:

- Professional independence and objectivity.
- Truth and accuracy.
- Professional competence.
- Compliance with technical and professional standards.

Throughout this book 'creative' is used in the sense of 'constructiveness' and 'objectivity', in order to meet a specified objective: namely, the provision of cost information pertinent to the needs of the user. This is consistent with the conclusion of the Accounting Standards Board's 'Corporate Report' (1975), when it said,

> In our view the fundamental objective of corporate reports is to communicate economic measurements of, and information about, the resources and performance of the reporting entity useful to those having reasonable rights to such information.

To conclude this introduction and to highlight some of the tasks/imponderables facing the cost and management accounting function, here are a selection of questions and quotes:

- What is cost?
- How best should costs be classified?
- How should stocks of raw materials, work-in-progress and finished goods be valued for costing purposes?
- How are the appropriate accounting concepts to be applied for costing purposes, e.g. materiality, conservatism, etc.?
- Is it really possible to divide certain costs into a fixed element and a variable element, e.g. labour?
- Which method/costing technique should be used?
- Which methods should be employed to apportion overheads to departments?
- Can costs be pre-determined with accuracy?
- How should service department costs be dealt with?
- Should we opt for absorption costing or marginal costing?
- Do the assumptions relating to break even analysis apply to the real world of business?
- Can realistic inter-firm/inter-departmental comparisons be made?
- Is it possible to place a fair valuation on a by-product or joint product at the point of separation?
- Will our budgets create behavioural problems?
- At what price should products be transferred from one group company to another?
- Can normal standard costs really be set?
- Which methods should be used for presenting data?
- How can management ensure that they have acquired all the relevant facts?

Now for the quotes:

> Our fixed overheads are a given amount.

> Sales growth and profitability do not always go hand in hand.

> Companies have withdrawn profitable products simply because of the way in which the products were costed!

> Budgetary control is all about comparing one inefficient performance with another inefficient performance!

> This particular product is making a loss so it must be eliminated from our product range.

Our standard costs are based upon normal working.

Companies should use marginal costing.

Beyond marginal cost is a world of make believe!

Companies should use absorption costing in an attempt to ensure that all costs are covered.

Creativity in cost and management accounting may be aided by the terminology.

Summary

The cost and management accounting function plays an important part in an organization's decision making process. Although the provision of information for decision making purposes represents just one of its areas of activity, it is an area in which there is great scope for creativity.

With cost and management accounting, it is necessary to rely on subjective judgement with greater frequency than is the case with financial accounting. This, along with various other factors, means that the behavioural consequences must be considered very carefully. The human element cannot be ignored. It is important to note that if the function does command the position of 'gate keeper' (Fig. 1.1), i.e. able to control the flow of information, its creative ability will be enhanced.

The objectives which this book attempts to achieve are, briefly, to encourage a more critical approach; expose unsound practices; create a greater awareness of limitations; encourage more time and thought to be devoted to the setting of objectives; provide a structure against which management can specify and evaluate costs; and promote the quest for more sophisticated techniques.

However, it must be stressed from the outset that cost and management accountants should strive to maintain their professional standards, e.g. as laid down in the UK and the USA.

We highlighted that the word 'cost' is very difficult to define and capable of a number of interpretations. In our opinion there is really no such thing as 'cost' and that cost is what it is defined to be and depends upon what it is to be used for!

The questions and quotes, many of which conflict, generate numerous other questions, e.g.
- What is normal and/or abnormal?
- In materiality, what is significant?
- In budgeting, can the future be predicted with accuracy?

Thus it can be observed from the material presented and the vast array of conflicting questions and quotes that there is great scope for creativity in the area of cost and management accounting.

Final quote: **'Beware accountants at work'**

2

Costs and cost classification

Cost accounting has been defined by the American Accounting Association (1959), as:

> The application of appropriate techniques and concepts in processing the historical and projected economic data of an entity to assist management in establishing plans for reasonable economic objectives and in the making of rational decisions with a view toward achieving these objectives. It includes the methods and concepts necessary for effective planning, for choosing among alternative business actions, and for control through the evaluation and interpretation of performance. Its study involves consideration of ways in which accounting information may be accumulated, synthesized, analysed, and presented in relation to specific problems, decisions, and day-to-day tasks of business management.

This definition emphasizes that cost accounting strives to provide pertinent information to a firm's management. Its non-use of the word 'cost' is indicative of the word's many meanings. Rayburn (1986) said that 'cost' was a term used for the measure of the efforts associated with manufacturing a good or providing a service. She said that there was no one 'true cost' of a good or service unless there is only one good or service being produced or rendered, and that there were different costs for different purposes. She also emphasized the use of the cost information when she argued that the type, purpose, and nature of a cost outlines its usage. The word 'cost' is generally used with other descriptive terms which define some characteristic of the cost measurement process or an aspect of the object being measured.

Similarly, Horngren (1977), said that 'there are different costs for different purposes'. He emphasized that the collection of cost data should be based upon some common wants for a variety of decisions. However, he also qualified the use of the cost data collected, since 'historical costs in themselves are irrelevant' to decision-making, although they may be the best available basis for predicting future costs. He also distinguished between 'qualitative' and 'quantitative' factors, in the decision-making process. He pointed out that cost data is associated with the quantitative factors, rather than valuing qualitative factors.

Rotch and others (1982) also emphasized that the 'correct' cost figure would depend on the specific circumstances and the intended use of the information. They pointed out that the dividing line between the different cost categories are often difficult to draw, and that the nature of a particular cost element changes depending upon the time frame under consideration.

We do, in fact, contend that there is no such thing as 'the cost' of anything, and that cost is what it is defined to be!

In cost and management accounting many costs are computed. The fact that they are computed and presented to management tends to attribute to them:
- A perceived high degree of accuracy;
- An air of respectability;
- An encouragement to others to do likewise and employ similar techniques.

Bourke (1969) concluded that:

> No single concept of cost is valid under all circumstances. We need different cost constructions and income concepts for different purposes. Costs take on a useful meaning only in relation to the specific objectives for which they are accumulated.

Kollaritsch (1979) felt that valuation was probably managerial accounting's most problematic task.

> Values are not absolute; different values may be required for different purposes, and some values are difficult to establish with any degree of accuracy.

The views expressed by Bourke (1969) and Kollaritsch (1979) highlight the need for clearly defined objectives in terms of the purpose for which the cost is needed. The purpose for which the cost is needed will help determine the way in which a particular cost is to be computed.

Cost and management accounting may be divided up between historical costing, i.e. costing after the event, and predetermined costing, i.e. costing before the event (Fig. 2.1).

It is not recommended that historical costing should be used for decision making

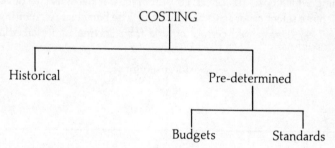

Fig 2.1   The principal types of costing

purposes. It looks backwards not forwards. Past performance is not necessarily a good predictor of future performance! Organizations which use historic costs for comparison purposes are quite likely to make no adjustments for the effects of inflation. They are also quite likely to be making a comparison between one poor performance and another poor performance without knowing it! The fact is that it is difficult to ascertain whether a historic performance is good, bad or indifferent! The historic costs are the actual costs. However, when it comes to the costing of goods and services, there exists a wide selection of actuals which could be used! Decisions will have to be made re:
- The method of pricing materials.
- The treatment of certain labour costs, e.g. over-time payments.

- The absorption of overheads, e.g. rent and rates.
- The treatment of administration, selling and distribution costs.

One would have thought that with the historic actual costs there is no scope for creativity, but there is! The accumulation of the historic cost of goods and services can only take place after making numerous choices and trade offs.

The items referred to above apply equally to pre-determined systems. It is, therefore, important that when comparisons are made between budgets and actuals that both sets of figures have been computed the same way. This is not always the case. With pre-determined systems material prices/quantities, labour rates/hours, overhead expenses and revenues have all got to be estimated. This is not an easy task. Various perceived assumptions about the complex environment in which the organization operates will have to be made. At least pre-determined costing in the shape of budgets and/or standards provide targets to aim at. Target setting can be quite a creative activity! Targets can and do affect the behaviour of individuals/groups of workers.

We believe that the creative use of cost and management accounting either intentionally or unintentionally has been responsible in whole or part for:
- Closing down a factory or department.
- The discontinuance of profitable products.
- Causing employees to strike.
- Encouraging employees to leave.
- Variances between employer's figures and trade union figures relating to the same event.
- The under/over pricing of goods and services.
- 'Window dressing', i.e. making the performance look better or worse than it really is.

In establishing which costs to collect, consider etc., it is necessary to develop criteria against which the selection of costs can be made. The Financial Accounting Standards Board, USA (1979) proposed certain criteria for selecting and evaluating financial

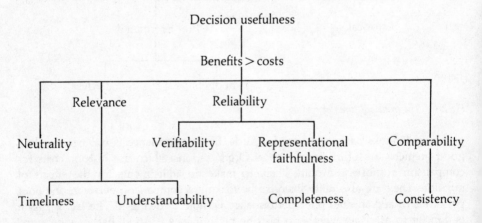

Fig 2.2 Hierarchy of qualitative characteristics

accounting and reporting policies. Belkaoui (1983) organized these criteria into a 'hierarchy of informational qualities', shown in Fig. 2.2.

Belkaoui went on to point out that cost accounting did not only rest on accounting but also on organizational structure, behavioural factors and decision-making foundations. He contended that:

1 The elements of the organizational structure may affect cost accounting's techniques, approach and role in a firm.
2 Cost accounting's explicit aim to positively affect the behaviour of individuals will require its adaptation to the different characteristics shaping the 'cognitive makeup' of individuals within an organization, and affecting their motivation to perform.
3 In order to facilitate and support an organization's decision-making, it is necessary to be aware of the kinds of decisions involved.

Shah (1981) took a more simplistic view of the areas to be considered when evaluating the management needs which should be satisfied by the cost objectives. He considered the following to be the key areas:
- Cost control.
- Profit determination.
- Price quotation and determination.
- Costs of designing, implementing and operating a cost system.
- Nature of the business.
- Data-base for profit planning, budgeting, and decision-making.
- Financial accounting and reporting.

Kollaritsch (1979) felt that the first steps should be the identification, definition and classification of the elements of business activities. Having established these 'data objects', their aggregation into a manageable classification should result in the establishment of 'cost objectives'.

Cost classification

Different authors have used different classifications of cost data. Drury (1985) said that there were many different ways of classifying costs. He emphasized that costing was the process of determining the cost of doing something, and that the objects of costing were always activities. He divided cost objectives into three broad categories, within which he distinguished between different aspects of costing, namely:

1 Costs for 'stock valuation', within which he distinguished between:
- Expired and unexpired costs.
- Period and product costs.
- The elements of manufacturing costs: material labour and overheads.
- The costing processes associated with job and process costs.
2 Costs for 'decision making', where he placed emphasis on future rather than historical costs, and distinguished between:
- Cost behaviour – in relation to the volume of activity.
- Relevant and irrelevant costs
- Sunk costs.
- Opportunity-costs.
- Incremental and marginal costs.
3 Costs for 'control', within which he distinguished between:
- Controllable and non-controllable costs.

- The appropriate methods of controlling variable or fixed costs via budgetary control procedures.

While Drury emphasized the use to which the costing data was to be put, in classifying costs, Rotch and others (1982) emphasized for what costs are provided, namely, by function, organization, and product or service. Within each of the three main categories, costs may be direct or indirect (to the cost objective), and/or variable or fixed in relation to the level of activity. Where it is necessary to focus on certain characteristics important to sound expense controls, they suggest that three sub-categories should ordinarily be used.

Engineered Costs

These are by definition those cost elements for which it is possible to determine or prescribe 'what the cost should be' for a unit of output or a given level of activity. Thus in a manufacturing operation where time studies, work methods, etc. have enabled the development of standard costs or standard times, a system of manufacturing cost control can be employed such that actual expenses are compared with 'standard' or 'allowed' expense.

Managed Costs (or Discretionary Costs)

For these costs it is not possible to prescribe 'what the proper costs should be' for a certain amount of output or for a given result. Consequently one cannot say whether actual spending is too high or too low.

Committed Costs

These costs are fixed, pre-determined, allocated or protected from cost-cutting. Examples: depreciation, certain contractual items.

Horngren (1977) classified costs by those costs relevant to particular classes of decisions. He classified costs between:

1 Costs that behave differently with changes in the level of activity, that is, costs which are variable, semi-variable, or fixed in relation to the level of activity.
2 Unit and total costs.
3 Product and period costs, which should be sub-divided between:
    (a) Manufacturing and non-manufacturing activities,
    (b) The three major elements of a manufactured cost, namely, direct materials, direct labour, and indirect manufacturing overheads.

This distinction would enable the matching of the cost of goods sold, with the revenue of the period in question.

Dudick (1985) emphasized the composition of costs (material, labour and overheads), and (like Rotch and others) the different cost systems available – job and process costing using actual or standard costs, and/or variable or absorption costing.

Shah (1981) classified costs by three aspects of a costing method, which he considered to be:

1 The production process or service orientation.

2 The time factor orientation.
3 The cost composition orientation.

Belkaoui (1983) merely listed different cost classification schemes at a more detailed level, rather than by broad groupings. In essence he captures the various classifications used by the other authors. His nine classifications were:

1 The *natural* classification – direct material, direct labour, manufacturing over-heads.
2 The *time* when the costs are computed, for example, historical or standard costs.
3 The degree of *averaging*, that is, the method of costing (job or process).
4 The *behaviour* of cost in relation to the volume of activity – variable, fixed, semi-variable.
5 The classification by *management function*.
6 The ease of *traceability* to the object of costing, that is, whether the costs are direct or indirect to the cost objective.
7 The *degree of control* of the costs by management.
8 The *timing* of charges against revenue, that is, distinguishing between product and period costs.
9 The relation of the cost to *managerial policies*, that is, are the costs committed or discretionary?

It is, therefore, obvious that there are many different classifications to which cost data can be designated.

CAN THE CLASSIFICATION OF COSTS BE CREATIVE?

The short answer is, a definite yes.

The application of accounting concepts such as 'matching' and 'materiality' will affect the figures produced, e.g. costs classified as expired, unexpired, period costs, time based, product costs, etc. A company may, at its year end, possess significant stocks of stationery, cleaning materials and advertising literature. However, both the financial and cost and management accountants may decide to write them off rather than carry them forward to the next accounting period.

In absorption costing the non-identifiable costs, i.e. those costs which cannot be identified with a cost centre, have to be apportioned to cost centres by way of technical estimates or some arbitrary basis. The insurance of buildings may be apportioned according to floor area, cubic capacity or the estimated value of the buildings occupied. In this particular area, which will be covered in greater depth later on, there are many choices which have to be made.

In the real world it is not always easy to distinguish between fixed, variable and semi-variable costs. The rent paid out for a machine is regarded as a fixed cost, whereas a machine rental based upon output is regarded as a variable cost! It must also be remembered that in the long term all costs are variable. Thus, exactly which costs are treated as fixed or variable is a matter of judgement. This area will also be considered in greater depth later on.

It is also difficult to identify certain costs with specific functions, e.g. selling, distribution and administration. Here also, it may be necessary to apportion certain costs using a wide selection of bases.

With product costing, the way in which products are costed will affect product profitability. The cost and management accountant and his/her staff do exercise a considerable influence over the success or failure of certain products.

A misconception that sometimes arises where costs are divided up into controllable and non-controllable, is that management may regard the non-controllable costs as a no go area. The truth of the matter, however, is that management can, by their actions, affect non-controllable costs. The cost of a machine break-down could be described as non-controllable. This could have been the result of poor servicing, inadequate maintenance, using an unskilled operator, etc., all of which could be sorted out by management action. From the creative viewpoint it is important to note that the terminology used can be knowingly or unknowingly creative. In the above example the use of the word non-controllable could well lead to management inaction!

Many of the other cost classifications, e.g. relevant or irrelevant, opportunity cost, productive or non-productive etc., rely heavily on the subjective judgement of the cost and management accountant and his/her staff. They have to decide if, why, when, where and how, such costs will be computed and used. They are the cost creators!

Summary

Cost accounting seeks to provide relevant information which should, if possible, be based upon quantitative data. However, this is not always the case and cost accountants and their staff are frequently involved with the assessment, interpretation and utilization of qualitative data.

The debate about what is cost was continued. It was noted that cost depends on the specific circumstances and intended use (Rayburn 1986 and Horngren 1977). The need to specify objectives was also highlighted (Rotch and others 1982).

The fact that costs are computed adds to the perception that such costs are accurate, acceptable and worthwhile. The fact that certain techniques are used, however relevant, promotes their use!

Historic costing is not so useful for decision making purposes and comparisons of actual results with historic costs can be pretty meaningless. With historic and pre-determined systems, decisions/judgements have to be made concerning material pricing, the treatment of labour costs and the absorption/non-absorption of over-heads. Pre-determined systems depend upon the perceived assumptions regarding the internal/external environment in which the organization operates. It is useful to set targets, but one must not lose sight of the fact that they are based on estimates and could well affect the behaviour of employees.

We believe that creative cost and management accounting has been wholly or partly responsible for closing down factories or departments, discontinuing the production of profitable products, causing strikes, encouraging employees to leave, variances between figures based on the same information, under or over pricing and 'window dressing'.

Cost accounting does not just depend upon accounting but also on organizational structure, behavioural factors and decision making foundations (Belkaoui 1983). The needs of management, which ought to be satisfied by the cost objectives, are divided into key areas, e.g. cost control, profit determination, price quotations, etc. (Shah 1981).

There are numerous cost classifications. However, the principal objective of this section was not to compile a mass review of the literature relating to different ways of classifying costs, hence the small sample. The principal aim was to illustrate how the process of cost classification can be creative. Some of the reasons why certain cost classifications may be classed as being creative are as follows:

- The application of accounting concepts, e.g. materiality and matching.
- The treatment of overheads, e.g. the selection of methods of apportionment.
- The problem of distinguishing between fixed and variable costs.
- The difficulty of identifying certain costs with a particular product, function, location/cost centre.
- Misleading terminology, e.g. non-controllable.
- The degree of subjective judgement.
- The interpretation of qualitative data.
- The use of historic data.
- The fact that pre-determined costs are estimates.
- Perceptions, assumptions and behavioural factors.

Decisions have to be taken about cost objectives and the way in which a particular cost will be computed. Decisions have to be taken about the way in which costs will be classified. The ascertainment of costs and the classification of costs are creative activities.

Part 2

The elements of cost

Introduction

It is suspected that quite a number of the providers and many of the users of cost data are not aware of the limitations.

A brief encounter with the elements of cost illustrates the problems facing the cost and management accounting function in their quest for realistic costs.

The chapters in Part 2, therefore, will consider the various elements of cost (material, labour and overheads, including manufacturing, administration, selling and distribution overheads) and their relationship to (a) the cost objective, (b) the level of activity, and (c) stock valuation (raw materials, work-in-progress and finished goods).

Dudick (1985) demonstrated that a substantial element of manufacturing companies' income is expended on 'manufacturing costs', although it varied from circa 90% for motor vehicles, to less than 40% for cosmetics. He also showed how the composition of manufacturing costs varied across different types of manufacturers. The results of his survey are shown in Appendix B.

It has been pointed out by various other authors – including Challos (1986), Brimson (1986), Pyne (1986), Keys (1986), Giacomino and Doney (1986) – that new production technology has changed the relationship/significance of the different elements of the production cost structure. Raw material and direct labour is less significant, while fixed manufacturing costs have increased significantly.

3
Materials and creativity

Material costs are separated between those which are direct and those which are indirect to the cost objective. In some instances certain material may be directly related to the cost objective, but excluded from the 'cost' because its value is considered insignificant. Indirect materials are incorporated into 'overheads'.

Material cost must be specified in terms of:

- The physical specification may be a 'standard' (i.e. what should be used: this requires a statement of the assumed manufacturing method, and manufacturing performance), or an 'actual' (i.e. what is used: this requires a statement of 'when', and under what circumstances this was achieved). Both should incorporate any 'losses' resulting from manufacturing wastage, either because of design or failure to conform to the specification.

- The value of each unit of material used, will depend upon the accounting pricing method adopted, and the treatment of stores losses, transport-in costs, and material handling costs. The pricing method adopted for the valuation of stock for costing purposes is usually at the discretion of the cost and management accountant. The method selected can have quite an impact upon the value of stocks of raw materials, work-in-progress, finished goods and services, for both historic and pre-determined costing systems. There are a multitude of methods from which the selection has to be made, e.g.
  - (a) FIFO: First In, First Out.
  - (b) LIFO: Last In, First Out.
  - (c) Average: Various methods, e.g. simple average, weighted average, periodic average, etc.
  - (d) Replacement cost.
  - (e) Standard cost.
  - (f) Others: NIFO (Next In, First Out)
                   HIFO (Highest In, First Out).

Dudick (1985) compared the three most common methods of pricing materials put into stock: first in, first out (FIFO), last in, first out (LIFO) and average cost. Using sample data for periods of falling prices, and for periods of rising prices, he showed that the deviations are greatest for the FIFO method, with the weighted average close behind. The LIFO deviations run fairly close to the zero line and show the smallest deviations. This means the use of LIFO will result in the least amount of distortion in product costing from period to period. The rate of change was somewhat large in the purchase prices used in these comparisons and this tended to exaggerate the deviations.

It is beyond the scope of this book to enter into a detailed discussion of the advantages and disadvantages of the above-mentioned methods. Suffice it to say that most costing texts devote adequate coverage to this area. The important points to note however, are:

(a) A choice of method has to be made.
(b) The method selected depends upon the opinion of the selector.
(c) The method selected will affect the value assigned to stocks of raw materials, work-in-progress, finished goods and services.
(d) The methods are perhaps better described as methods of pricing materials issued rather than methods of valuation.
(e) With some of the methods, an attempt to have realistic product costs means unrealistic valuations of raw material stocks and vice versa.

It must also be remembered that inflation does affect stock holdings and stock replacement. Decisions need to be made about the treatment of holding gains on raw material stocks and how to account for inflation in product costs.

Then there is the problem of dealing with damaged and/or obsolete stock. An assessment of the degree of damage and whether or not stock is obsolete can be a highly subjective activity!

Another decision which has to be made is the treatment of scrap and waste. This could well have a significant impact on the figures produced.

The 'cut-off procedure', i.e. the procedure which decides whether or not stock which arrives just before the year end will be included in stock valuations, may be adjusted as necessary!

It is accepted that pricing methods/costing treatments should be applied consistently from period to period. However, the method used can be changed as and when desired! Thus, meaningful periodic comparisons of material costs may in practice be extremely difficult.

The foregoing notes are evidence of the fact that when it comes to the costing of materials there is most certainly great scope for creative cost and management accounting. Stock valuation will be discussed in greater depth in Chapter 7.

Mini cases of creativity in the area of materials costing

1 HOW NOT TO FIX THE STANDARD PRICE OF A COMPONENT

The cost office found out that they had no standard price for a particular component. One member of their staff went along to the buying office to find out what the standard price should be. On being asked, the buyer simply looked at a price list and said, 'Oh, call it £26.75 each.' Not very scientific! However, it does highlight the point that the fixing of standard prices is not always done with the care and attention which it deserves. Thus, without knowing it those responsible were being creative. On the other hand, it must be remembered that standard material costs are only estimates and also that their computation may be quite creative.

2 WHEN OBSOLETE STOCK IS NOT OBSOLETE

An organization had a policy of only scrapping a pre-determined percentage of obsolete stock each year. In years where the actual amount of obsolete stock exceeded the percentage which could be written off, the excess was simply carried forward at its historic cost. Not very good accounting and quite a silly system but nevertheless, creative!

3 STOCK LEVELS WERE TOO HIGH

The stock levels at a company's year end were expected to be too high. The value of the stock was reduced by the following manoeuvres:
  (a) All stock considered to be obsolete was written off.
  (b) All damaged stock was written down.
  (c) The 'cut-off procedure' excluded from the stock-take all stock coming in after 20 December 19x7.
  (d) Certain stock was sold at cost to another company. This stock was then bought back in January 19x8.

This example of 'window dressing' in action, made it possible for the company to reduce its stock valuation by a significant amount. It must also be noted that the decision as to whether or not stock is obsolete and the assessment of the degree of damage is dependent to a large extent on subjective judgement. Some of the obsolete stock written off was subsequently found to be not obsolete and written back in February 19x8!

4 COMPETITIVE QUOTATIONS

The management accounting section of a company knew full well that to succeed, their quotes had to be very competitive. Thus, the material content of the job for which they had to quote was priced on a FIFO basis. This illustrates that the objective, i.e. making a competitive quote, was the prime factor in the selection of the pricing method. The cost of material content is a very important element in computing quotations, pricing decisions and make or buy decisions.

Holding costs

In addition to the cost of the stocks of raw materials, fuels, work-in-progress and finished goods, there are also holding costs.

WHAT ARE HOLDING COSTS?

Unfortunately, there are too many rules of thumb and not enough hard facts published on what constitutes holding costs. Holding costs include: the cost of the capital tied up; the costs of the storage space, e.g. rent, rates, insurance, light and heat, etc.; administration costs; etc. etc. The following article is just one attempt at answering what turns out to be quite an open ended question.

THE COSTS OF HOLDING STOCKS
In addition to having vast sums of money invested in stocks of materials, fuel, work-in-progress and finished goods, British industry has also to cover

expensive holding costs. In the first of this two part article the author attempts to answer the question: 'What are holding costs?' – a question frequently ignored by accountants and others, probably as a direct consequence of the difficulty of quantification. If problems are being encountered by management in establishing how much their holding costs are, then it follows that even greater problems arise, when one asks: 'How can the value and volume of stocks held be reduced?'

When asked the question 'how do people set a value on the cost of holding stocks?' one eminent purchasing executive replied 'This is a question to which I have never really found a satisfactory answer. I have posed the question to numerous accountants and the net result was one that could only be described as useless from the point of view of practical application'.

It is rather surprising that many accountants are not particularly interested in this very important area when especially one considers the substantial amount of working capital tied up in stocks of materials and fuel, work-in-progress and finished goods (Table 1).

The stocks held at the end of 1978 by manufacturing industry were a staggering £30.7 bn (around 56% of UK stocks). Figures of this magnitude illustrate how important it is to control stocks effectively.

Table 1   Source – National Income and Expenditure 1979 Edition

The distribution of UK stocks
(at the end of 1978)

		£bn	%
Manufacturing:	Materials & Fuel	10.7	19.4
	Work-in-Progress	11.7	21.3
	Finished Goods	8.3	15.1
Agriculture		4.9	8.9
Wholesale Trade		7.2	13.1
Retail Trade		5.7	10.4
Other Industries		6.5	11.8
		55.0	100

In most industries the cost of material forms a significant part of the final selling price of the product.[1] Management must not only strive to increase the productivity of labour but must also endeavour to increase the efficiency of Material Requirements Planning (MRP) and thereby improve the productivity of capital. ROI (Return on Investment) is the real name of the game of business. The cost profiles of British Industry indicate the importance of materials (Table 2).

Thus, other than increasing the selling price which may be sensitive to competition and external factors, materials management may, by direct inventory reduction and increased efficiency, play their part in increasing the productivity of capital employed.

The principal aim of materials management is to keep stocks at an acceptably

Table 2   Source – MRP and The Organisation by JBS Houlihan[2]

The average cost structure of British industry sales

	%
Materials	56
Labour	23
Overheads	14
Profit	7
	100

low level consistent with the risks involved.[3] However, stock outs can cost the firm dearly in terms of lost production, idle time and lost orders. The setting of stock levels and levels of service must therefore involve a trade-off, hence the need for up to date information, continuous monitoring and frequent review.

Holding costs
What is the cost of holding stocks in your company/industry?

A rule of thumb puts the cost of holding stock for one year in the region of 25p for every £1 of stock held.[4]

The rule of thumb does indicate that holding costs comprise a significant portion of business expenditure. However, it must be remembered that there will most certainly be quite wide variations between the holding costs of companies and industries.

Which figures need to be included in the calculation of holding costs? It can be observed [Fig. 3.1] that holding costs of stocks include the costs of acquisition, storage, controlling, handling and rehandling, administration and others such as insurance and financial charges, and all these are in addition to the cost of the stocks held.

Acquisition costs
The principal cost in the procurement of bought out stock items is the cost of the purchasing function which is made up of staff wages and salaries, office accommodation and equipment and overheads, e.g. light and heat, telex and telephone, stationery etc. All the costs of ordering, finding suitable suppliers and negotiating terms should be included.

Receiving department costs of personnel and resources used for receiving and inspection of goods inwards may also be classed as part of acquisition costs.

The stores – warehouse function
The stocks of raw materials, work-in-progress and finished goods all take up valuable factory space in terms of expense and scarcity. Factory and office space is nowadays an extremely expensive commodity and must be utilized efficiently. The overheads associated with the space used for storage are many and include: rent and rates, insurance of buildings and equipment, light and heat, fire prevention, cleaning and maintenance. To this must be added the wages and salaries of stores and warehouse personnel. There is also a substantial investment in stores – warehouse equipment, e.g. bins and racks.

In addition there are also losses attributable to shrinkage, deterioration, obsolescence and pilferage to consider.

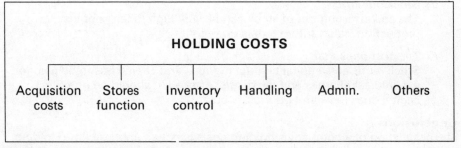

Fig 3.1   The costs involved in holding stocks

Inventory control
A lot of time and effort should be devoted to this area in order to keep stock levels to an acceptable minimum and thus bring about savings in holding costs.

The costs applicable to this area involve material requirements planning, monitoring and review, the chief element being manpower. The expenditure upon internal audit related to stock control should also be included under his heading. The cost-benefit of the system of inventory control should not be overlooked.

Handling
There could well be quite a hefty investment in handling equipment, e.g. overhead cranes etc. In addition to the capital outlay for such equipment further expenditure has to be incurred to cover running costs, maintenance and servicing, e.g. drivers' wages, power fuel and lubricants.

Administration
It may be more appropriate to include certain expenditure which could quite rightly appear under this heading, under some other heading, e.g. management of purchasing and material requirements planning. However, the costs of the financial and cost accounting recording systems for stocks acquired/issued and payments to suppliers must be accounted for.

Others
  (*a*) *Insurance*
      Insurance premiums paid out to cover stock losses cannot be ignored. Insurance premiums are almost certain to rise when a firm increases the value of the stock it holds during the year. As pointed out already insurance must also be taken out to cover buildings, equipment and other risks, e.g. employer's liability and public liability.

  (*b*) *Set-up costs*
      Where a company manufactures some of their own components this involves a number of other costs in addition to the direct materials and labour, e.g. setting costs, machinery, patterns etc. and an appropriate share of overheads.

  (*c*) *Imported materials*
      Various fees, duties, freight charges, and foreign exchange management relating to the importation of stock comprise yet another addition to the calculation of holding costs.

(*d*) *Stock out costs*
The cost of being out of stock can be very high in terms of lost production, sales, future orders and profit.

(*e*) *The cost of capital*
Stock represents capital tied up in goods and capital has to be paid for, e.g. interest charges and dividends. After all, it should be noted that capital does have an opportunity cost.

Conclusions

The calculation of a company's holding costs is not an impossibility. Holding costs can be identified and classified under a number of headings [Fig. 3.1]. However, without actually calculating a company's holding cost it is almost certain that a vast sum of money is expended in this area and that because there are numerous variables the holding cost is unique for each individual company.

Companies do keep an analysis of their payroll and materials used and should therefore be in a position to calculate with accuracy some of their holding costs. Overheads can be allocated and apportioned to departments/cost centres according to established cost accounting practice.

It must be remembered that as stocks increase in volume, value and variety the complexity of management planning and control also increases, and thus holding costs escalate.

BIBLIOGRAPHY

1   Lockyer, K. G. *Factory and Production Management.* Pitman.
2   Houlihan, J. B. S. Proceedings of 13th BPICS European Technical Conference, 1978, 103.
3   Oliver, S. *Accountant's Guide to Management Techniques.* Gower.
4   Ray, D. L. *Inventory Management Performance Must Improve.* Purchasing and Supply Management, April 1980.

Summary

The application of the accounting concepts can and does affect the treatment of materials. The pricing method selected at the discretion of the cost and management accountant, e.g. FIFO, LIFO, Average, etc. affects stock valuations for both historic and predetermined costing systems. It must, therefore, be noted that a choice of pricing method has to be made and that the method selected could include trade-offs, e.g. realistic product costs v. unrealistic stock valuations for raw materials and vice versa.

Decisions have to be made re the treatment of:
- Inflation,
- Damaged and obsolete stock,
- Scrap and waste.

Creativity can also be aided by the application of 'the cut off procedure' and the degree of consistency applied in the materials costing area.

From a study of the mini-cases it should be clear that:
- Standards should be set with care (mini-case 1).

- The treatment of obsolete stock can reduce or increase the stock valuation (mini-case 2).
- 'Window dressing', in addition to being used in financial accounting, may also be used in cost and management accounting (mini-case 3).
- The reason why a cost is needed could determine the way in which it is calculated, be it right or wrong! (mini-case 4).

The computation of an organization's holding costs also involves a number of choices. Many permutations of what constitutes holding cost are available. Quite a number of important decisions may rest on the computation of holding costs. The article on the subject which has been reproduced in this chapter highlights the difficulty of calculation and provides much food for thought. For many organizations it is quite likely that their holding costs may be far greater than envisaged!

Much of what has appeared in this chapter also applies to financial accounting. However, to the extent that cost and management accounting is not as constrained by company law and SSAPs (i.e. Statements of Standard Accounting Practice) as financial accounting, it is our considered opinion that it provides even greater scope for creativity. Much of what has been produced for costing purposes will have to be re-computed for financial accounting purposes. Where does it say that costings which are used for internal purposes have to give a true and fair view?

4

Labour and creativity

Labour may be considered direct or indirect to the cost objective. 'Indirect labour' has been defined in terms of the work performed by the individual and/or the element of pay to an individual. For example, a general labourer may be considered indirect to a manufacturing operation, although direct to the manufacturing function. Whether or not his/her cost could be considered direct to a product would depend upon the actual work he/she performs and/or whether only one product is produced in his/her work area. Those labour costs which are regarded as indirect are treated as overheads. Thus, there is scope for creativity right from the outset, because a decision has to be made as to whether a particular labour cost is to be treated as direct or indirect. The distinction is not always clear cut, e.g. an employee may be involved directly in the production process but remunerated via a fixed wage or salary.

It is often assumed that 'direct labour' can be considered an expense that varies with the level of production. In so far as direct labour is defined as that time spent on producing products, then its treatment as a variable expense is not unreasonable. Direct labour is essentially an allocation of 'direct workers' labour costs to a cost objective. The total pay of direct workers may or may not be variable, depending upon the output 'steps' one is relating to, the manufacturing requirements, and operator efficiency.

In some instances, only certain elements of a direct worker's pay is deemed 'direct'. For example, overtime premium may be considered indirect because it may be impossible to decide upon which cost objective it should be allocated to. For example, it may be allocated to the cost objective being worked on in overtime, or the cost objective(s) which caused the overtime to be worked!

The actual productive labour hours, i.e. the time spent transforming raw materials into finished goods is a matter of fact and so is the actual rate paid. The budgeted/standard productive labour hours and the budgeted/standard labour rates are matters of fantasy! Yes, budgets/standards are only estimates and yet they form an important part of the data upon which decisions are made. Quotations, selling prices and make or buy decisions all depend upon the adequacy of the pre-determined costs for materials, labour and overheads. Thus, the cost of the labour content of product costs can also be regarded as a creative element. In computing the direct labour cost, decisions will have to be made about the treatment of the following:

- Employer's national insurance contributions.
- Overtime payments.
- Incentives, e.g. bonus payments/setting piece rates, etc.

- Payments for shiftwork and unsocial hours.
- The division between variable and fixed elements.
- Idle (or non-productive) time, e.g. waiting for work.
- Rectification work.
- Setting time.

The answer to the question, 'What constitutes the direct labour cost?' is, various combinations of the above list. The combination being dependent upon whosoever is responsible for the way in which the thing is worked out!

The historic time analysis is not always a good guide of future performance. Performance is affected by the skill factor, industrial relations, behavioural factors and the reward system. It is a fact of life that organizations have to price products and make their quotations well before any sale takes place. The pre-determination of costs is, therefore, a necessary evil.

The cost and management accounting function plays a major role in the setting of piece rates and the formulation of incentive schemes. Creativity here tends to take the form of a balancing act. The rates/schemes have to be acceptable to management and workers/unions. Once fixed, the rates/schemes will affect the behaviour of employees and could result in either under or over production. Certain incentive schemes have caused employees to leave and have also been a prime cause of a high labour turnover. Another reason why creativity is possible in the area of incentives is that normal levels of activity and normal performance have to be defined. What is normal is a matter of opinion! Certain bonus schemes, e.g. annual bonus schemes in particular, may be instituted to aid cash flow. There is a time-lag between the end of the period to which the bonus relates and publication of the results, and yet another time-lag between the publication of results and the payment of the bonus.

Decisions have to be taken on how the idle (non-productive) time is to be analysed and its division into controllable and non-controllable causes. Examples of idle time are: waiting for work; waiting for materials; waiting for setter; machine breakdown; training new operatives, etc. The time spent training new operatives can be treated in a number of ways, e.g. ignored, employee estimated, a standard allowance, etc. The misconception relating to controllable and non-controllable was pointed out in Chapter 2 and the remarks made apply equally to the labour costing area.

The definition of direct work has many complications depending upon the manufacturing environment, the payment methods, the work performed by the individual, the system of manufacturing control, and the cost accounting system established. Two specific problem areas which must often be addressed are: the treatment of setting time, and where a direct worker operates more than one machine – often setting one while the others are working! Keys (1986) argued – in the context of using numerically controlled machines – that the criterion to be used for deciding whether labour should be considered direct or indirect is whether it 'can be easily and accurately traced to the product'.

Decisions which are influenced by the cost office must also be taken about the time recording methods employed, e.g. time sheets or cards, computerized time recording etc., and the contents of the payroll analysis. It is important to note that the way in which the payroll is analysed will be reflected in the costs which are produced. A direct worker's salary may be split up equally between two production departments. However, the truth of the matter could be that this was a true reflection of the particular worker's time allocation a few years ago, the current position being significantly different. It can be argued that the costing section is being creative by being inactive! Situations which are allowed to continue from year to year without a careful review can create a completely different picture to the one which really exists. Another point worthy of mention, is that the design of time recording systems may result in employee antics. Employees may abuse the system, e.g. inaccurate time recording. Employees can also be creative!

The costing section will no doubt be required to supply both quantitative and qualitative information for: job specifications, job evaluation, merit rating, flexi-time. This again puts them in a position of power and their role as a 'gate keeper' is further enhanced.

With budgets and standards numerous variables have to be considered and assumptions made about: the rate of inflation; pay rises; bonus earnings; the level of activity; times allowed for performing operations; strikes and disputes, etc.

The cost of labour turnover

The rate of labour turnover may be calculated as follows:

$$\frac{\text{Number of employees leaving in the period}}{\text{Average number of employees on the payroll for the period}} \times 100$$

What is the cost of labour turnover?

Here also there are many variables which could be included and qualitative factors to take into account. In practice it will depend upon those who calculate it and how they decide to calculate it. It can include the costs of: recruitment; advertising; selection; engagement; the personnel function; induction training; pre-job training; own training; training schools; courses; accidents; lost production; increased scrap. On the qualitative side an assessment needs to be made about the effect on morale and motivation.

Many cost and management accounting sections never attempt to compute their organization's cost of labour turnover!

Mini cases of creativity in labour costing

1 TO CHARGE OR NOT TO CHARGE!

The costing section were computing the labour costs for a batch of components and came up with the following figures:

Department	Direct labour hours	Labour rate per hour	Amount
		£	£
Machine Group A	6	7	42
Machine Group H	3	8	24
Assembly	2	6	12
		Labour cost	78

Was £78 correct? Upon further investigation it was found that in order to meet the delivery date the machine group H operative had to work over and was paid time and a half. The operative in machine group A took an estimated two hours longer than expected because of breaking off to help train a new operative. Rectification work had to be carried out on the batch involving two hours which were paid for at £8 per hour. The cost of the overtime and rectification could be charged in costing the batch and the cost of training the new operative could be excluded: the decision rests with the cost and management accountant and his/her staff. The above case used quite simple figures; in practice the figures involved could run into thousands!

2 SERVING A SECRET OBJECTIVE!

Once upon a time there was a medium sized private limited company. Trading conditions had deteriorated over the past few years. The company secretary, in consultation with the costing staff, devised a new bonus system in order to improve productivity. After a trial period of two months it appeared obvious to all concerned that the incentive scheme was most unsuitable. The management insisted that the scheme be retained. In the words of the company secretary, 'We know that there are problems with the incentive scheme but it is the only way forward'. As a result, quite a number of employees became disillusioned and left to find employment elsewhere.

Had the real objective been to reduce the labour force?

If targets are set too high employees may just opt out of trying to achieve them. If targets are too low groups of workers may agree between themselves about production levels and may even build up hidden stocks!

Finally, it must be remembered that the cost and management accounting section will no doubt be actively involved in the selection, review and implementation of remuneration systems.

Summary

This chapter was chiefly concerned with direct labour, i.e. that labour which is used to transform raw materials into finished goods. The distinction between direct and indirect labour is not always clear cut. Yet, a decision has to be made whether to treat certain types of labour as direct or indirect. The choice rests with the cost and management accounting section.

Standard and budgeted labour costs are only estimates and depend upon the quality of the data which was utilized when they were being prepared. Labour hours, labour rates, the labour content of jobs/products, all have to be pre-determined using the best available information. The cost and management accounting section enjoy great freedom of choice when it comes to the preparation of standards and budgets.

Decisions have to be taken about remuneration systems and the treatment of numerous variables, e.g. employer's national insurance contributions; overtime payments; incentives; shiftwork payments; fixed and variable elements; idle time; rectification work and setting time.

Incentives, standards and budgets can affect the behaviour of individual employees or groups of employees.

A single chapter could have been devoted to the question, what is the cost of labour turnover? However, this was outside the scope of this book. Its cost is difficult to calculate because, it would appear, there is no general agreement as to which items should be included. Its attempted computation will therefore, be subjected to a high degree of creativity. We believe that it is a cost which is frequently overlooked and an area in which more research is needed.

The charge or not to charge mini-case illustrates that the choices open to the cost accountant enable him/her to become more creative.

The second mini-case is a fictitious story which indicates that the cost and management accounting section can, via the figures they produce, e.g. incentive schemes, affect the behaviour of employees. In this particular example the scheme was developed to achieve a specific objective, i.e. to reduce the labour force! Extremely creative!

5
Direct expenses and creativity

Robotic costing

More and more robots are being employed in the production process. How are their costs to be incorporated in product costs? If the robot is purchased outright its original cost is a fact. However, because of advances in technology its life and any residual value are uncertain. Thus, any attempt to compute the annual cost (depreciation) of the robot is going to be difficult and will be dependent upon the views of the cost and management accounting section.

A robot engaged in the production process can be treated as a direct expense. In some ways its working life is similar to that of direct labour, i.e. some of its time spent in the factory will be productive and some, when it is not operating, non-productive. In truth therefore, it should really only be the productive time that is classed as a direct expense, but this is just a matter of opinion. A decision would have to be made re the non-productive time, e.g. treat as overheads. It would also have to be decided whether or not the cost of servicing and maintenance should be included as part of the robot's annual cost or as an overhead.

How will the cost, i.e. depreciation, of the robot be charged to a job or product? The cost may be apportioned via machine hours, direct labour hours, etc. Note that the base used has to be estimated. It is our opinion that a more accurate method could use the estimated productive and non-productive hours to split the cost up between direct and indirect. The direct portion would be charged to production on an hourly basis, the indirect would be included with the overheads. However, in a few years' time we may in fact favour dealing with it in some other way! As times change, so do our views and our capacity to be creative.

The above arguments can also be applied to purchased machinery, plant and equipment which is used in the production process.

Sub-contract work

Sub-contracting is frequently treated in the same way as direct material. The goods/components resulting from a sub-contract agreement are very similar to bought-out-finished goods/components. Not much room for creativity! Wrong!

In the first instance the costing section has to produce figures to justify the cost of employing sub-contractors. More time spent on supplying better information re machine utilization could, in fact, have identified ways in which idle capacity could have been used and the use of sub-contractors unnecessary.

Decisions have to be taken as to whether the cost of fixing up a sub-contract agreement or transport costs to and from the sub-contractor should be included as part of the sub-contract cost.

In the UK public sector the sub-contracting decision is highly political. It should be noted that it could be possible to produce figures which either support or reject the sub-contracting alternative! If fair comparisons are to be made in the public sector it is essential that standard methods of computation be developed.

The hire of machinery, plant and equipment

The fixed asset which has been hired could be subject to a fixed charge or a charge which varies with output. In the first case, even though the cost is fixed, the extent to which the asset is used in the production process is really a direct expense. The comments made in relation to robotics re productive and non-productive time apply equally here. In the second case there is a definite link between the hire charge and the production. The hire charge would be treated as a direct expense.

It should be noted that from a financial accounting viewpoint, it is very difficult to compare the accounts of companies who own most of their fixed assets with those companies who have a substantial involvement in sub-contracting and the hire of fixed assets.

Power

Costing texts do devote some space to debating whether or not power should be treated as a direct expense. They tend to agree that power used in the production process is a direct expense but because of measuring difficulties could be apportioned to production in the same way as an indirect expense. It is our view that, because of advances in technology, it should be possible to assess power consumption per department, per machine, per product, etc. with reasonable accuracy. In some firms the power generated is also used to provide light and heat and this does present problems. Advances in technology, e.g. low cost meters/computers, etc. should assist in overcoming the problem, e.g. to ascertain the heating consumption per department/cost centre.

Carriage

Carriage inwards (i.e. on purchases) tends to be treated as part of the material cost and is therefore a direct expense. It is, however, difficult to get a realistic carriage inwards figure because in a lot of cases carriage is included in the price paid for the materials and not disclosed as a separate item on the invoice.

Carriage outwards (i.e. on sales) may be included with all the other distribution expenses and either apportioned to products in the same way as overheads or written off to the Profit and Loss Account. On the other hand, it may be a relatively simple task to relate the carriage charge to a particular product. Carriage outwards could be treated as a direct expense.

Other expenses

The key factor to the direct versus indirect saga is identifiability. Can the expense be identified with the product? This will affect the cost accounting treatment of items such as royalties and sales commission payable.

When is a direct expense an indirect expense?

- Certain direct expenses are so insignificant in value that they are simply lumped together as overheads (i.e. indirect expenses).

- When the cost and management accountant and his/her staff direct otherwise!

Mini cases of creativity in the direct expenses area

1 IDENTICAL MACHINES – DIFFERENT COSTING TREATMENT

Three companies in the same industry hired identical machines to produce the same products. The terms of the hire agreements were as follows:

Company	
L	£20 000 per year
E	£20 000 per year
S	£1 per unit produced

Company L treated the £20 000 as a fixed cost and added it on to the overheads of the cost centre concerned.

Company E, while recognizing the £20 000 as a fixed cost, also recognized the fact that it was still a direct expense which could be identified with the products. As a result, its cost was included in product costs at a rate per unit produced, based upon the estimated number of units to be produced.

Company S treated the £1 per unit as a direct cost (i.e. a variable cost).

The terms by which the hire charge is paid affects the direct versus indirect decision here, identifiability being ignored in the case of company L.

2 WHO IS RIGHT?

The company's management accountant produced figures which showed that it would be better to close down a particular department and sub-contract the work involved to SC Ltd. The employees affected were not convinced. They secured the help of their trade union. The trade union's accountants produced some figures for them which showed that sub-contracting would be more expensive.

It should be noted here that the two accountants were producing costs for different objectives. The amusing thing about this case is that if other accountants were asked to compute figures it is quite possible that they could come up with significantly different results!

The sub-contracting decision

The following article incorporates two cases which indicate that there are quite a number of non-financial factors involved in the sub-contracting decision.

THE SUB-CONTRACTING DECISION
A large number of undertakings, in the public or private sectors of the UK economy, employ the services offered by sub-contracting road haulage companies.

Why sub-contract the distribution function?

There are several reasons why companies sub-contract all or part of the distribution function. The principal advantages are as follows:

- *Financial* The employment of sub-contractors frees the user of the service from having to find large sums of money with which to purchase essential fixed assets. Thus, fixed assets such as buildings for warehousing offices and garaging purposes, vehicles, fixtures, machinery and equipment, e.g. ramps, tools, etc. would all be provided by the sub-contractor.

  The absence of such fixed assets means that the user will not have to keep stocks of fuel for vehicles, spare parts for vehicles, machinery and equipment, and materials for cleaning and maintenance of premises.

  There would also be considerable savings in labour costs. In addition to not having to pay wages and national insurance to drivers, warehouse, garage and stores personnel, there would be other savings. Such savings would be attributable to the costs which would have had to be incurred in areas such as: payroll preparation; the personnel function – recruitment and selection; welfare – health care, sickness schemes, canteen; training and labour turnover, etc.

  A vast amount in overheads would also be saved. Financial charges, e.g. interest on money used to finance new fixed assets and stock holdings, would be avoided. Other holding costs associated with the acquisition, control and management of stocks would also be saved. Lighting, heating, cleaning and maintenance costs of the fixed assets, e.g. buildings and vehicles would not have to be paid out. Many other expenses would not have to be found, e.g. licences; insurance of vehicles, premises and stocks; printing and stationery; accountancy charges and administration costs.

- *Practical* One reason for utilizing the services of the sub-contractor is simply size. A company may be just too small to attempt to provide its own distribution function. As mentioned earlier the resources necessary, in terms of fixed and current assets, labour and overheads could be quite substantial.

  The location of a company's outlets may make it impossible to serve all areas of the UK and Europe. Sub-contractors may therefore be engaged to deliver small consignments to areas in which the company has infrequent deliveries and/or a small market share. Companies will have to decide upon their intended levels of service to customers in various areas and make their distribution arrangements accordingly. Thus, the employment of sub-contractors means that a company can have a wider customer base.

- *Organizational* Distribution is a specialized functional area. It needs to be planned, co-ordinated, reviewed and therefore needs the appropriate management skills. The engagement of a sub-contractor enables those organizations who are weak in this area to buy-out the services which they require. This enables them to concentrate their efforts in the areas in which they enjoy a differential advantage over their competitors, e.g. production, research and development, etc. They will not have to worry about all the legal matters relating to health and safety regulations and drivers' hours, etc. Freedom from red-tape can provide a lot of time for doing other things and contribute towards the business being a successful one.

So, why not leave it to the experts?

The advantages appear to put a very good case for the sub-contracting of all/some of a company's distribution function. The realities of the matter are that sub-contractors have to cover their own costs, and such costs will be reflected in the prices quoted. However, the possible employment of sub-contractors should be very carefully considered and one needs to shop around to find a quality service at the right price.

What could go wrong?

The answer to this question is best illustrated by two short cases from the real world of business.

Case 1   A Southern depot – a trial run
After careful consideration, X Ltd, a distribution company in the Midlands, in an attempt to improve its services to the south east of England entered into a sub-contracting agreement with Z Co. Ltd.

Z Co. Ltd is a small family run company based south west of London, specializing mainly in international haulage. To complement their international work they also had a small vehicle for forwarding smaller consignments of goods which they had brought into the country. Their vehicle park and garage is in a separate location to the office. If storage facilities were required they rented part of a small warehouse which was, again, in a different location to the office and garage.

The system which was operated was that X Ltd would still deliver in North London but any goods for South London, Kent, Sussex, Surrey and Hampshire would be taken to the warehouse used by Z Co. for them to deliver. A second van was obtained by Z Co. to cope with the extra work.

Goods were sent each morning from X Ltd to Z Co. and a list of those goods was sent to Z Co. on the telex. Then, as goods were being unloaded at Z Co.'s warehouse the consignments were checked off against the telex and a signature obtained by the X Ltd driver. The Delivery Instruction notes were retained by Z Co. who then planned the routes to be followed by their vehicles the next day.

At the end of each month the costs and revenues were allocated to each consignment. The overheads incurred by each company were then taken into account and the profit, or loss, was divided equally between the two companies.

The experiment came to an end sooner than expected for a number of reasons. One major unforeseen fault with the operation was the image of Z Co. as perceived by many of the X Ltd employees. For a service such as this to succeed it needs the complete backing of the companies concerned. Z Co. had in the past done international work for X Ltd and occasionally problems had arisen which were considered by some of X Ltd's employees to result completely from Z Co.'s incompetence and inefficiency. Whether or not this is true is unimportant. The fact that rumours and opinions had been widely spread and had subconsciously affected some of the people involved with the new service, both at managerial level and in the warehouse, meant that not everyone in X Ltd was enthusiastic about the link.

Another problem was the high costs involved, especially at the Southern end of the operation. In the estimation of many people at X Ltd, some of whom were ardent supporters of the link, some of the costs submitted by Z Co. were excessive. For example, they declared as part of their overheads the full cost of employing a person to run the operation (who was actually already working for Z Co. before the service began) when the work involved probably only occupied two or three hours of his working day. High vehicle costs also resulted from the fact that the drivers were given the decision as to what time to return to the depot at the end of the day, regardless of whether they still carried undelivered goods. Consequently consignments were often returned which meant that less goods could be put on the van next day. This resulted in increased delivery costs per consignment. Apart from increased costs it also led occasionally to complaints from customers that their goods took longer to deliver.

Early in the life of the service an X Ltd vehicle was sent down to Z Co. for them to use for their deliveries. The aim of this was to save them the cost of acquiring another vehicle at the same time as having the X Ltd name seen around the delivery area. However, two different vehicles were sent down there for a month each, for the first two months of the project, and, much to the surprise of X Ltd both were rarely used. Apart from the loss of use of the vehicles which resulted it caused more negative feelings at X Ltd towards Z Co.

Problems also arose concerning the balance of work provided by each company. At X Ltd it was considered that Z Co. were not working to promote the northbound service from their area, and that the effort was purely one way. At one point the X Ltd distribution manager spent several days in the southern area visiting potential customers with the Z Co. manager. However, he gained the impression that the only service being fully promoted was that which Z Co. could offer internationally. In the later stages of the operation it also came to light that Z Co. had never done as much UK work themselves before. It was also found out that due to Z Co.'s work on the continent not being as busy as usual they had been using their own vehicles to deliver to, for example, the Midlands. At the same time they explained to X Ltd that all of the loads concerned were too large for X Ltd's vehicles. It seemed from this that the impression gained by X Ltd's distribution manager was correct and, once contacts had been made, Z Co. benefitted mostly from them.

Yet more problems arose in the level of communications within Z Co. itself between its different sites. If someone in the office wished to contact someone in the warehouse this had to be done via the telephone in the office of the company from whom the warehouse was rented. Also, at the vehicle park and garage, where the manager spent a large proportion of his time, the only means of contact was to telephone the people who lived next door and rely on their goodwill to forward a message. This system was obviously lacking and, even if contact was made, it was very slow and time consuming.

The most major problem of all was the geographical position of the Z Co. facilities. They were based to the south west of London and experience revealed this to be the wrong side. When the service was originally started it was hoped that as it developed X Ltd trailers from the continent would clear customs at the port and deposit any consignments bound for London and the South East at the Z Co. depot on their way to the Midlands. However, because of the standard of roads leading to the warehouse, and the routes available from Dover, it was almost as quick for them to go straight to the Midlands. The ideal geographical position would be to the south east of London near the M2 (the Dover to London motorway) so that continental vehicles would not have to go out of their way.

The sub-contracting agreement was terminated in the first half of 1984.

Fortunately for X Ltd this did not signify the end of their southern service because immediately Z Co. withdrew another possible opening appeared.

Case 2   Sub-contracting to Y Ltd

X Ltd were left with the goods which still needed delivering to south east England. Y Ltd were contacted and a meeting held to discuss the situation. It was decided that X Ltd would sub-contract their south east England distribution to Y Ltd. It was hoped that there would be reciprocal work from Y Ltd, which was bound for anywhere north of London.

The system of operation was that X Ltd delivered the goods to Y Ltd (near Dover) and then Y Ltd would distribute them on their own vehicles. This connection had satisfied at least one of the major faults of the link with Z Co. in that, geographically, it was better situated and with good access to northbound motorways. Also, if the link was developed further it was ideal for immediate distribution as they came off the ferries. If anything was wrong geographically it was that Dover was too far away from London and was at the eastern extreme of the area X Ltd goods were being delivered to.

Once again major problems arose. In the effort to maintain their southern service the agreement was almost rushed into and, for example, Y Ltd had delivered goods on behalf of X Ltd before a final rate scale was agreed. As far as X Ltd was concerned the prices charged were much too expensive. In fact, in some cases Y Ltd wanted more for the final delivery than customers were paying X Ltd for the whole job. Throughout the life of the project this problem was never resolved.

The promises of reciprocal work from Y Ltd were well meant, but such work was not forthcoming.

A further problem which arose was that of the vehicles returning purely at the discretion of the drivers when they felt they had done enough. Due to the fact that Y Ltd were situated at the eastern extreme of the delivery area, and that all their drivers had families in and around Dover, they often turned around for home at a certain time regardless of where they were and what was left on the vehicle. If similar things happened each day goods destined for the western extremes of the region covered by Y Ltd could be left undelivered for days. There were obviously many complaints due to the slowness of the service. In one particular case, when some goods were required for loading on a ship for export, the ship sailed without them after Y Ltd had had the goods for almost a week and had failed to deliver them.

The link lasted less than two months and, when broken, still left X Ltd with goods to deliver to the south east of England.

Conclusions

- Hindsight is a wonderful thing; everyone can be wiser after the event.
- The cases which are based on real life situation illustrate firstly the need to draw up carefully thought out and clear agreements covering all of the aspects of the situation. One must not rush into this type of agreement:

even a short experimental period could prove costly. Legal advice may save a lot of money in the long term.

- Management must satisfy themselves at the outset that any reciprocal arrangements will in fact be honoured.
- The location should be subjected to a more detailed investigation. Proximity to the market and access to the motorway network are, nowadays, of prime importance.
- If a company provides a very good service to Europe, it does not follow that their UK operations will also be very good. The quality of the service required should be critically evaluated, assessed and if possible, tested.
- The attitudes of employees must be right, so that they accept and support any links with sub-contracting distribution firms. The right attitude can make or break a contract.
- Sub-contracting of a company's distribution function however, remains as a practical option which is available to large and small alike. Provided that the terms are right, and that the sub-contractor's services match expectations, you are not just buying a service but also convenience and peace of mind.

Summary

The cost of employing a robot may be classed a direct expense. The cost of the robot is quite difficult to ascertain because advances in technology create uncertainty about the asset's life and residual value. It also has to be decided upon whether or not to include servicing and maintenance as part of the robot's cost.

There are a number of methods which can be used to charge the robot's cost to production, e.g. machine hours, direct labour hours, productive and non-productive hours etc.

Creativity arises in the sub-contracting decision because figures have to be supplied which justify the use of sub-contractors. In the UK public sector this is a highly political and emotive area. The sub-contracting decision also involves numerous non-financial factors.

With the hire of fixed assets for production purposes the terms of the hire could in fact determine whether or not the expense is treated as direct or indirect! This is illustrated via mini-case 1. The machines are identical, used in the same industry, used to produce the same products, but the cost accounting treatment varies from company to company!

To those who argue that power used for production purposes is a direct expense and then advise treating it as indirect because of the difficulty of measurement, we have a message. Please remember that nowadays that inexpensive meters and computers can be used to obtain accurate readings.

Other problem areas concern the treatment of carriage, royalties and sales commission in the direct versus indirect classification decision. The key being traceability, i.e. identification with the product.

Treatment does depend on the application of the accounting concepts and the wishes of 'the cost and management accounting section.

Mini-case 2 once again points out that the objective for which the figures are prepared can affect the way in which those figures are computed!

6

Overheads and creativity

The area of overheads perhaps provides the greatest scope for creativity. The way in which overheads are estimated, allocated, apportioned and absorbed may have a significant impact upon the survival of production departments, service cost centres, goods and services. The treatment of overheads most certainly does affect decision making and in many instances has been the major cause of a wrong decision! In the public sector the overhead apportionments cause political friction and conflict, e.g. the apportionment of central administration costs to departments/cost centres.

Overheads are those costs which are considered not directly attributable to cost objectives. However, since cost objectives are established at different levels of detail, it is often found that the definition of direct is related to the lowest level of detail, which is often the product. Costs relating to, for example, a specific group/range of products are often classified as indirect.

Various issues are raised in this area such as: the usefulness of actually allocating costs; the bases of apportionment; the establishment of 'cost pools'; the bases of absorption/recovery to the different cost objectives; and the level of activity relevant to the costs.

The usefulness of allocating costs

In a study published by the NAA, Fremgen and Liao (1981) found that

> Despite the overwhelming objections to indirect cost allocations found in the literature, most companies responding to the survey reported charging corporate indirect costs to their primary profit centres.
>
> Blanchard and Chow (1983) contended that allocating and apportioning indirect costs to responsibility centre managers can reduce 'budgetary slack' and induce greater goal congruence between the firm and its managers. They demonstrated that allocating indirect costs at a 'standard' rate, based upon the budgeted/forecasted data provided by the divisional manager, can reduce the amount of 'budgetary slack'.
>
> Zimmerman (1979) observed that even when a corporate service involved only fixed out-of-pocket costs, increasing use of this service by organizational sub-units can still entail increasing costs to the firm as a whole, because of delays/degradation of service. If one assumed that the use of a service entails incremental costs to the firm, charging for the service could lead to a more optimal utilization of the resource. A lump sum charge would not satisfy this objective, since users would still view the cost of an additional unit as zero. Thus the user charge must be related to usage.

Rotch and others (1982) held that the rationale used in choosing a base for allocating/apportioning overhead usually considers the following criteria:

- *Benefit*: the department that receives the most benefit is charged the most, e.g. maintenance.
- *Variability of usage*: if overhead varies with a measure of activity, that measure of activity is used as a base.
- *Traceability*: if an item of overhead can be traced to a department, even though benefit and variability may be indistinguishable, that department is charged.
- *Fairness*: for some overhead items there is no clear benefit, variability, or traceability. In these instances whatever method seems fair is generally used.
- *Simplicity*: a complex procedure is often both expensive and confusing. Sometimes the simplest way is best.

The Establishment of cost pools

The term 'cost pool' is often used to describe any grouping of individual costs. Subsequent allocations are made of cost pools rather than individual costs. Costs are frequently pooled by department, but they can also be pooled by natural categories (for example, materials related or people-related) or by behaviour pattern (for example, variable or fixed costs). The idea of aggregating or pooling costs is the result of abandoning ideal cost-allocation schemes for cost benefit reasons. There is a need to ensure that the costs included in a pool are homogeneous.

Overhead pools and allocation bases are sometimes subdivided because of the difference between the behaviour patterns of variable and fixed costs. For example, variable costs are often allocated in proportion to the short-term usage of the allocation base, whereas fixed costs are sometimes allocated in proportion to a longer term 'availability' (such as 'normal' usage or 'peak' requirement) regardless of short-run fluctuations in usage.

A key issue is the reason why a service department has been established, with the facilities it has! However, the answer may lie in history, and have no relevance to the current circumstances. Or it may be, as Horngren put it, 'equipped because of the whims of the president'.

The bases of absorption/recovery to different cost objectives

When products are heterogeneous, receiving uneven attention and effort as they move through various departments or cost centres, departmental or cost centre overhead rates are necessary to achieve more accurate product costs. In these situations, the departmental rates are frequently described as being more homogeneous than plantwide rates.

Homogeneity refers to all ingredients of the cost allocation rate, both within and between the numerator (the cost pool) and the denominator (the cost apportionment base). That is, defects in either the numerator or the denominator can result in a non-homogeneous average cost rate. For example, the summing of recruiting costs and data-processing costs and dividing by machine hours is likely to be non-homogeneous because (a) the costs in the pool have a little commonality of purpose, and (b) the apportionment base has no direct causal relationship to these costs. The testing of homogeneity may lead to:

- Redefining the cost objectives, because there is no need to discriminate among them.
- Choosing a different apportionment base, because in testing we discover another base that will yield a more acceptable level of homogeneity (a better cause-effect fit).
- Choosing different cost pools.

The level of activity relevant to the cost

Grinnell and Mills (1985) quoted from a survey by Chiu and Lee of Fortune 500 companies, to discover what activity level types were used in establishing fixed overhead rates. They found that these different methods were used by the respondents:

- *Expected activity* (= budgeted activity) – 58% of the respondents;
- *Normal activity* (= year-on-year average of expected activities) – 18% of the respondents;
- *Practical capacity* (= the maximum level at which the plant or department can operate efficiently = capacity available for use) – 21% of the respondents.

They also distinguished between 'committed' overheads and 'managed' fixed overheads:

> 'Committed' overheads are those costs which are necessary to sustain production activity over an extended period of time, and are not subject to alteration in the short-run; examples of this type of cost are depreciation on plant and equipment, property taxes, etc.
>
> 'Managed' fixed overheads are those costs which are subject to periodic adjustment by management, usually on an annual basis. While these costs do not bear a well-defined relationship to volume of activity, they typically must be budgeted at a level necessary or desired to support the expected operating activity over the next year; examples of this type of cost include non-key supervisory personnel, employee training programmes, etc.

They recommended that the managed overheads should be recovered on the 'expected' activity, and the committed overheads on the 'normal' level of activity. They developed a view that for external reporting purposes the use of the 'practical capacity' level of activity may be justified.

Absorption costing v. marginal costing

Management have to decide whether to use an absorption costing system or a marginal costing system. Their decision will no doubt be based upon the information supplied and the views put forward by the cost and management accountant.

Absorption (or total) costing either allocates or apportions all/most (hence the name total costing) overheads to cost centres and eventually absorbs them in product costs via an appropriate absorption (recovery) rate, the principal aim being to ensure that all costs are covered. Creativity arises because:

- The overheads have to be predetermined.
- The bases by which the overheads, which cannot be identified with a particular cost centre, are apportioned, e.g. floor area or cubic capacity etc. have to be selected.
- The method by which the service department overheads are apportioned must be selected from a number of alternatives.
- The absorption (recovery) rate has to be selected and certain figures estimated, e.g. direct labour hours and/or machine hours etc.
- Decisions have to be made on the treatment of administrative, selling and distribution overheads. Absorption costing is dealt with in greater depth in Chapter 8.

Marginal costing distinguishes between variable costs (i.e. those costs which vary with the level of activity within a relevant range) and fixed costs (i.e. those costs which do not vary with the level of activity within a relevant range). To distinguish between fixed and variable costs is not always an easy matter. Marginal costing treats the fixed costs as 'period costs', i.e. they are written off in the period in which they are incurred. They are not therefore carried forward to future accounting periods via stock valuations. This will be considered in more detail in Chapter 9.

Summary

Of all the areas with which the cost and management accounting function come into contact, the area of overheads perhaps offers the greatest scope for creativity. This is true for both private and public sector organizations. The treatment of overheads may, in fact, create much strife and conflict!

This chapter was really just an introduction to overheads and creativity. The treatment of overheads is an absorption (i.e. total) costing environment is discussed in greater depth in Chapter 8. The marginal costing treatment of overheads is considered in Chapter 9.

The way in which overheads are dealt with can lead to the provision of information which is: considered, used and relied on as a basis for decision making. However, the information provided was not prepared with the decision making objective in mind and may be quite unsuitable for such a purpose. The cost and management accounting function may be guilty of being creative without knowing it! They innocently produce product costs which is an attempt to recover overheads and then permit those costs to be used for decision making purposes.

Creativity arises in the computation of the pre-determined overheads, the allocation of costs, the selection of apportionment bases, the treatment of service department costs, the selection of absorption (recovery) rates, the treatment of administration, selling and distribution costs.

From a brief review of the literature it is clear that:

- Many companies do, in fact, use absorption costing (e.g. Blanchard and Chow, 1983).
- The charging for services (which is not an easy task) is intended to lead to a more optimal use of resources (Zimmerman, 1979).
- The allocation and apportionment of overheads should take account of the benefit received, variability of usage, traceability, fairness, and simplicity (Rotch and others, 1982).
- There are different levels of activity which may be used (Grinnell and Mills, 1985).

The treatment of overheads does have a dramatic impact upon the imputed costs of cost centres' goods and services.

7

Stock valuation and creativity

The valuation of stocks of raw materials, fuels, work-in-progress (including long-term contracts) and finished goods, is yet another area in which a high degree of creativity is possible. Much of what has been said already in relation to materials, labour, direct expenses and overheads applies to the valuation of stocks, e.g.

Materials:
>   Pricing systems.
>   The 'cut off procedure'.

Labour:
>   The decision on whether the labour is direct or indirect.
>   The treatment of overtime.

Overheads:
>   The selection of the methods of apportionment.
>   The selection of the methods of absorption.

In the UK the valuation of stock incorporated into a company's balance sheet is guided by the Statement of Standard Accounting Practice 9 (SSAP 9), and the Companies Act 1985. In the preamble to SSAP 9 it was stated that:

> No area of accounting has produced wider differences in practice than the computation of the amount at which stocks and work in progress are stated in financial accounts. This statement of standard accounting practice seeks to define the practices, to narrow the differences and variations in those practices and to ensure adequate disclosure in the accounts.

Thus, even after adoption of the standard, differences and variations will occur. The issue was not seen to be about which basis stocks should be valued on, for 'historical cost', as distinct from 'current cost', was taken as given. The issues were seen to resolve themselves via a fairly technical discussion as to which element of historical cost should be incorporated into the value of inventory.

Griffiths (1986) recognized the scope for creativity, when he wrote:

> The audit of stock is undertaken with the same fear, care and apprehension which is normally found amongst bomb disposal experts.

SSAP 9 (para. 26) defined stocks and work-in-progress other than long-term contract work in progress, as:

The amount at which stocks and work in progress, other than long-term contract work in progress, is stated in periodic financial statements should be the total of the lower of cost and net realizable value of the separate items of stock and work in progress or of groups of similar items.

Creativity could follow, therefore, along three lines:
- Cost definition.
- The calculation of net realizable value.
- The grouping of stock items.

Cost definition

Cost was defined in relation to the different categories of stocks and work in progress as being that expenditure which has been incurred in the normal course of business in bringing the product or service to its present location and condition. Cost was said to have four elements:

1 'Cost of purchase', which comprises the purchase price per unit, plus import duties, transport and handling costs, and any other directly attributable costs, less trade discounts, rebates and subsidies. The scope for creativity is perhaps limited to how one could 'reasonably' apportion the transport and handling costs, and the general rebates and subsidies. General rebates may be 'averaged' across all purchases or allocated to those marginal items which initiated the actual level of rebate received.

2 Costs of conversion: conversion costs are costs which are specifically attributable to units of production, i.e. direct labour, direct expenses, and sub-contracted work. Creativity is largely restricted to the definition of direct labour. The technical specification could be varied according to:

(a) The operations defined as direct. For example, while a machining operation may have a clearly defined 'time', the process time of, say, a heat treatment operation, may not be so closely defined and a labour cost rate not so easy to calculate.

(b) The time used: a pre-determined time may be a 'theoretical standard' or a 'current estimate' based on current practices, or a standard with various 'allowances' for non-100% performance; while an actual time may or may not include setting time or some non-productive time.

The labour rate per hour may be defined in a number of ways:
- Basic hourly paid rate.
- Total gross pay divided by the actual hours worked.
- Total gross pay + direct labour overheads, for example, National Insurance payments in the UK, divided by the actual hours worked.
- The above 'pay definitions' divided by, for example, actual direct hours worked, or 'standard hours produced'.

3 Production overheads: SSAP 9 (para. 20) defined these as:

overheads incurred in respect of materials, labour or services for production, based on the normal level of activity, taking one year with another. For this purpose each overhead should be classified according to function (e.g. production, selling or administration) so as to ensure the inclusion in the cost of conversion of those

45

overheads (including depreciation) which relate to production, notwithstanding that these may accrue wholly or partly on a time basis.

Appendix 1 of SSAP 9 recognized that problems arise in the allocation and apportionment of overheads. Their selection/usage will usually involve the exercise of personal judgement.

Creativity may derive from:

(a) The bases of apportionment used to attribute to the different manufacturing centres. Furthermore, Appendix 1 of SSAP (9 para. 42) accepts that:

where management accounts have been prepared on a marginal cost basis, an appropriate proportion of production overheads not already included in the marginal cost should be added

The calculation of a global 'add-on' offers an opportunity for creativity.

(b) The costs deemed to be manufacturing costs. Although 'General Management' is specifically excluded from the cost of conversion (SSAP 9, Appendix 1, para. 38) where a General Manager is involved in functional activities, for example, manufacturing, the cost of management may be fairly allocated to, for example, manufacturing (SSAP 9, Appendix 1, para. 39). Although a central service may in general terms be considered an administration function, for example, the Accounts department, SSAP 9 Appendix 1, para. 40 explicitly allows an element of the Accounting department's costs to be allocated to production.

(c) The level of the company's 'normal level of activity'. Para 41 of Appendix 1, SSAP 9, identified the following considerations as to what constitutes 'normal':

the volume of production which the production facilities are intended by their designers and by management to produce under the working conditions (e.g. single or double shift) prevailing during the year;

the budgeted level of activity for the year under review and for the ensuing year; and

the level of activity achieved both in the year under review and in previous years.

Although temporary changes in the level of activity may be ignored, persistent variations should lead to a revision of the previous norm.

The cost accountant can be creative by taking these 'considerations', which are largely internal management judgements, with different assumptions, e.g.

- The product mix may produce different 'production hours' despite a similar sales value or 'physical' measure of output.
- Production efficiency/performance.
- The degree of 'cost variability' with the level of activity, particularly in respect of the semi-variable 'stepped' costs.

4 Other overheads, if any, attributable in the particular circumstances of the business to bringing the product or service to its present location and condition. For example, where firm sales contracts have been entered into for the provision of goods or services to customer's specification, overheads relating to design,

and marketing and selling costs incurred before manufacture may be included in arriving at cost: SSAP 9, para. 35, Appendix 1.

It is often not practicable to relate 'costs' to specific units of stock and work-in-progress. In order to approximate to 'actual cost', then it is necessary to select an appropriate method:

- For relating costs to stock/work-in-progress, for example, job costing, process costing and standard costing.
- For calculating the related cost where a number of identical items have been purchased or made at different times, for example, average cost or FIFO.

SSAP 9 requires that:

> Management must exercise judgement to ensure that the methods chosen provide the *fairest* practical approximation to 'actual' costs. Furthermore, where standard costs are used they need to be reviewed frequently to ensure that they bear a *reasonable* relationship to the actual costs obtained during the period. Methods such as base stock and LIFO do not usually bear such a relationship (para. 45, Appendix 1).

Elsewhere SSAP 9 (para. 34) Appendix 1 requires that the actual costs should exclude all 'abnormal' conversion costs, which are avoidable under normal operating conditions. The failure to define 'fair', 'reasonable', or 'abnormal' leaves much scope for creativity. For example, does 'abnormal' exclude all manufacturing variances calculated in the management accounts? The answer will in part depend upon the definition of the standards used in preparing the management accounts. Where they have allowed for 'normal inefficiencies', then the answer could be in the affirmative. However, perhaps one could argue that the standards are now inappropriate, or that there were valid/acceptable explanations for the variances, which could quite 'reasonably' be incorporated (or not) into the stock valuation.

Calculation of net realizable value

Net realizable value (NRV) for 'finished items' is the net of the sale price of the item, less any customer/trade discounts allowed, less any additional cost to complete the sale, such as distribution or selling costs. Creativity could be expressed via assumptions re future customers and/or discounts to selling prices allowed, or the necessary distribution and selling costs to complete the sale. For items held as raw material or work-in-progress, NRV will also be reduced by the 'manufacturing cost' necessary to complete the item. All the opportunities for creativity identified above may be used re the additional manufacturing costs required.

The establishment of provisions by the use of formulae are not disallowed under SSAP 9. The formulae may take account of the age, movement during the past, expected future movements, and the estimated scrap values of the stock. Subject to the NRV criterion, these formulae, and their arbitrary provisions, are subject only to the cost accountant's creativity – and, perhaps, the auditor's need for 'consistency'.

Grouping of stock items

The grouping of stock items for valuation purposes, including the establishment of provisions, facilitates further creativity. In part, the grouping will result from an unsophisticated costing system or inventory count. In general, one would expect the less the information available, the greater the degree of potential creativity.

Stock value for costing purposes

It should also be noted that the value of stock for costing purposes is not always the same as the value for financial accounting purposes, e.g. standard costing systems, marginal costing systems etc. Thus, the provisions of SSAP 9 and the Companies Act 1985 can be totally ignored by the cost accountant when producing figures for costing purposes. There is great scope for creativity in the financial accounting stock valuation figures, but even greater scope in the cost accounting stock valuation figures!

Long term contracts

SSAP 9 (para. 27) states:

> The amount at which long-term contract work-in-progress is stated in periodic financial statements should be *cost* plus any *attributable profit*, less any *foreseeable losses* and progress payments received and receivable ... etc.

As mentioned in earlier chapters, it is especially difficult to define cost and the assignment of materials, labour and overheads may be highly subjective. The attributable profit also depends upon judgement and the amount of foreseeable losses can be difficult to assess.

Particular problem areas are also areas which are ripe for creativity, e.g.

- *Plant values.* The valuation placed on plant transferred to other contracts or returned to the depot before the year end and the plant which is still on the site at the year end can have a dramatic effect upon the cost of the contract. The assessment of plant values in the construction industry is not an easy matter and open to differing interpretations, even within the same company.
- *Stocks of materials.* A similar situation exists in the case of the valuation of materials returned to stores and those which remain on site.
- *The value of work certified.* The value of work certified to date may be the result of a compromise between the architects working for the contractee and the architects working for the contractor! This figure is important as it is frequently linked to the amount/s of cash that is paid on account. In order to ascertain a profit the cost of the work to date, certified and uncertified, has to be computed.
- *Conservatism* (i.e. Prudence). Because of the nature of the industry and uncertainty about the future, profits which are to be taken to the Profit and Loss Account during and at the end of the life of a contract tend to be scaled down (see (b)

below). Very creative! Paragraph 7 of SSAP 9 states that it is 'appropriate' to take credit for ascertainable profits. This raises a number of questions:

(a) How should the profit to date be calculated?

(b) How much of the profit to date should be credited to Profit and Loss Account (Prudence), e.g. 2/3 and/or $\times \dfrac{\text{cash received}}{\text{value of work certified}} \times \dfrac{\text{the profit for}}{\text{the period}}$

- *The outcome.* Paragraph 8 of SSAP 9 recommends that if the outcome of a long-term contract cannot be reasonably assessed before it comes to an end, then no profit should be taken and vice versa. Can the outcome be predicted with accuracy? This is a matter of opinion.

Mini cases

(For other mini cases relating to stock see also Chapter 3.)

1 CREATIVE ERRORS!

A company was unaware that it had some flaws in its application of the 'cut-off procedure'. At the particular year end in question, stock which arrived on or after the cut-off date was not included in the stock valuation. However, because of recording errors certain items which had not been included in the stock valuation were included in the purchases figure for the year. The effect upon profits can be illustrated by the following simple example.

Items excluded from stock but included in the purchases figure amounted to £18 000. Opening stocks and purchases excluding this figure amounted to £440 000. The closing stock (which excluded the £18 000) amounted to £56 000. Sales were £485 000.

	Correct figures		Error created figures	
	£000	£000	£000	£000
Sales		485		485
Opening stock plus				
Purchases	440		(+18) 458	
Less Closing Stock	56	384	56	402
Gross Profit		101		83

The error made an £18 000 difference to the profits!

Management must therefore see to it that the 'cut-off procedure' is working satisfactorily and if stocks are excluded from year end stocks that they are also excluded from purchases and creditors.

It must also be noted that there are many other errors which can take place when evaluating stock and work in progress (see the case of the half-a-million pounds stock deficit in Case 3 of this chapter).

2 SAME PLANT, SAME LIFE, SAME USE – DIFFERENT CHARGES!

Two contractors, M & Co. and P Ltd both purchased the same plant for £45 000 on the same date. In both cases the plant went direct to the respective construction sites. In both cases the plant remained on the site for nine months and was then moved on to another contract. An independent assessment of the condition of the plant would have revealed that the plant of M & Co. was in much better condition than the plant of P Ltd. Both businesses used the revaluation method of depreciation and the amount charged to each contract account was, as follows:

	M & Co. £000	P Ltd £000
Cost	45	45
less Value after nine months use (say)	20	35
Charge to Contract Account	25	10

It all depends upon who is doing the re-valuations! It can be observed from the above mini case that the re-valuation decision will affect the cost of the contract/profit on the contract.

Now for a longer case.

3   THE CASE OF THE HALF-A-MILLION POUNDS STOCK DEFICIT

A few years ago a large UK retail organization found that it had a stock deficit of over half-a-million-pounds*. It took a small team of specially selected personnel over two months to sort it out and their findings were quite revealing.

- What were the reasons for the stock deficit?
- What lessons can management learn from the findings?

One of the problems of being involved in a real life case study is that it happens in the real and diverse world of business and involves real people. Human beings are complex variables and in a given situation are most likely to react to it in different ways. The human element makes this unique case even more unique; human behaviour is certainly most unpredictable.

Any organization is bound to have its share of human problems and this particular organization was no exception. Each section seemed to be blaming the other for contributing to this apparent stock deficit. In particular managers and supervisors seemed to be on the defensive and very un-cooperative. It was also apparent that departmental sub-optimization was the rule. Departments tended to follow their own departmental goals and strove towards building up their own little empires. The problems created by sub-optimization are:

1   *Objectives*. The departmental goals followed may be in direct conflict with the organization's own goals.
2   *Conflict*. Empire building can lead to conflict between departments and weaken the three C's of communication, co-operation and co-ordination.
3   *Resource allocation*. It is highly likely that scarce resources may be wasted, e.g. the more powerful departments could well win resources which they do not really need.
4   *Departmental practices*. Some departments may, for their own convenience, institute practices which would be frowned upon by top management. In one of the departments of this case some stock returns were sent in on bits of paper without any proper control and this was considered by the departmental manager as being a satisfactory arrangement.

*A half-a-million pounds difference between the book stock and the physical stock.

In addition to the departmental sub-optimization the general *attitude* which prevailed amongst the senior staff was, that as the company's business involved the selling of goods via their sales outlets all their energies must be directed into getting the goods from the company's warehouses to their stores. This attitude of mind promoted in turn the attitude that stocktaking and documentation control take up too much time and are of secondary importance. Although this does have a ring of truth about it, it should be noted that a stock deficit of half-a-million pounds is a lot of money!

Falsification and human error

The team's energies were directed towards the opening stock balance of the year in question. The stock cards had been posted with the differences between physical and adjusted book stock to reflect the physical counts but all the cards were not posted correctly, there were many cases where debits were posted for credits and vice versa.

The amazing thing about all this was that, in spite of the incorrect postings of differences, the closing book stock for the current period was reconciled with the purchases ledger. Upon further investigation it was revealed that, the particular department concerned never balanced in spite of the production of tally rolls for opening stock. The clerk for this department confessed that after having spent a whole week trying to balance the stock accounts without any success, she forged the closing stock tally roll totals by overlapping the tally roll and pressing the total key, thus allowing the incorrect total to be punched and then subsequently chopped off. She then pushed the tally roll upwards to line up just under the last figure and punched in the results of the opening stock. It so happened that this latter total was the same as that on the purchases ledger. If this discrepancy was not picked up, it would have had the effect of doubling all those stock differences which were incorrectly posted and thus reflecting itself in the current year's stock figures even before any movements of stock. This accounted for £40 000 of the stock deficit. This item can be attributed to stress caused by the inability of the personnel involved to balance the accounts.

It is the responsibility of management to ensure that adequate systems of internal control are in operation. The company's own internal audit staff should ensure that systems are not only in force but also that such systems are working efficiently. Personnel should never be subjected to such a high degree of stress as experienced in this case. However, in addition to improving the company's internal control the company's staff education and training could also be improved.

There was no conventional method as FIFO or LIFO* used when valuing closing book stock, nor was there any consistency even in the haphazard method already in use. However, assuming a world without taxation and inflation, it does not matter what figure is used to evaluate closing book stock providing the same base is used to value physical counts. However, it does matter when the pre-stocktaking closing stock figures are computed with the side effects of price variances and particularly so when these variances are not adjusted for in the purchase ledger. Strictly speaking, the purchase ledger is part of the accounting system, book stock records are part of the management information system. When the physical counts were reconciled with the closing book stock figure and the differences posted onto the stock cards as well as the purchase ledger no action was taken with the price variances on

*FIFO—First In First Out and LIFO—Last In First Out are both well known methods of stock valuation.

the purchase ledger, this then produced an imbalance between the physical, book and purchase ledger figures. This price variance accounted for £30 000.

There were some clerical errors in adding and balancing each card although both the debit and credit side of the total columns agreed, this nevertheless accounted for about £25 000. There were also some compensating errors (i.e. errors that tend to cancel each other out).

The denomination of quantity

A closer inspection of the stock reconciliation sheets revealed that certain items of the adjusted book stock had a negative balance which is simply just not possible! Upon closer scrutiny it was discovered that there was a problem of misinterpretation of the invoice quantities. Bacon is normally invoiced to the company in quantities of sides of carcasses. Two sides make one carcass. However, a particular shipment was invoiced in quantities of whole carcasses, so in effect when it was cut up each carcass produced two forearms, two middles and two backs and not as before one forearm, one middle and one back. However, each cut has its own lot number and is put on three separate cards. When the consignment of 2000 carcasses arrived, each card should have shown 4000 units of each lot number but instead showed only 2000 on each. This in effect accounted for around £15 000 of the stock deficit.

The problem of denomination of quantity (D of Q) was significant and accounted for £104 000 of the deficit. D of Q is a unit of quantity: this quantity could be in 10s, 12s, 18s or 24s but the unit is still one. The fruit and vegetables department's invoices were booked in quantities of 12. However, the warehouse received certain produce in boxes of 18 and subsequently issued to the stores in the same box as one unit instead of one and a half units. This had the effect of showing a shortage in physical stocks when compared with the book records.

One problem which arose during the physical stocktake of merchandise was that the same lot numbers for the same items were recorded on various rough stock sheets because of the physical location of stocks. For the same lot number some of the rough stock sheets showed a D of Q of 6, 12 and 18. When these were collated and transcribed onto the master stock sheet it showed a D of Q of 12, thus although the physical count was correct, carelessness in transcription of the D of Q had created a deficit between the physical counts and the adjusted book stock figure.

The denomination of quantity is certainly an area in which great care must be exercised, not just in this particular case but in all businesses. The physical count must be in the correct denomination of quantity. The prices by which those physical stocks are multiplied must relate to the same denomination of quantity.

Example

Item No.	Description	Quantity	Price Per unit	Amount
			£	£
XY11932	socks	500	4	2000

On the face of it the above example appears correct but it isn't, in fact 500 pairs of socks have just been priced at £4 which is the price per dozen not the price per pair!

Management must therefore take greater pains to ensure that stock-takes are properly organized and carried out. A system of continuous stocktaking where a number of items are checked say daily/weekly could help resolve problems, avoid errors and save a considerable amount of time and effort at the year end.

The team specially set up to investigate the stock deficit had found that significant portions of it were attributable to human error, falsification, unposted price variances and problems associated with the denomination of quantity. They also encountered people problems which were reflected in working practices, departmental sub-optimization and the attitudes which had been formulated over the years. They faced a considerable amount of hostility from both managers and staff during the course of their investigation. However, their enquiries carried on regardless and eventually accounted for the deficit. Behavioural problems still persisted, attitudes and practices of working cannot be changed overnight, indeed in the large organization concerned one would envisage that it will take years to bring this about.

So, how then was the remaining part of the deficit made up?

Invoices paid twice

The investigation revealed that there was an invoice which had been paid twice. When the original invoice was received it was kept in the drawer of a clerk so that it could be processed. However, the following week the clerk went on holiday and in the meantime the supplier phoned for payment. The person who dealt with this query requested a photocopy because the original invoice could not be found. The normal procedure was carried out and payment made. However, when the clerk returned from holiday she took the original invoice, looked for the Goods Received Note (GRN) but could not find any as the original had already been processed. A request was made to the Warehouse for a photocopy, the normal processing was done and payment made again. The person recording the last posting on the stock card did not discover the error in spite of the commonality in the postings. This accounted for £37 000. Funny but it's true!

Duplication of Goods Received Notes

Duplication of Goods Received Notes although they do not normally affect the postings on the stock cards, nevertheless are incorporated in the accruals thus increasing the adjusted book stock figures and consequently create an adverse variance when compared with the year end physical counts. It was found that the information was on certain occasions given twice to the office for the same consignment and that this was particularly the case when there had been a change in shifts at the receiving bay. This has been further amplified by the lack of control on GRN pads (four pads were in use) and by the non standard information system whereby the GRN is raised. Duplicated GRN's which were included in the accruals accounted for £70 000 of the stock deficit. One consignment of merchandise which was received was documented, paperwork processed and invoice paid. Later it was discovered that the garments needed pressing. The consignment was then returned to the supplier and no Debit note was raised as it was felt then that since the consignment had been paid for it was unnecessary. The result was that originally this has been recorded as an input on the stock cards but was not taken into account in either of the physical counts or as accruals in the adjusted book stock figure, consequently a deficit of £30 000 has been recorded.

Some stock kept at outside warehouses was also not included in the physical counts as the owner of the warehouse moved part of the stock to another section of the warehouse because of repairs to the roof. No-one told the stocktakers about this, consequently goods to the value of £5000 were not included in the physical counts.

There were no damage reports made by the warehouse, although food items damaged were taken and used by the warehouse canteen. Merchandise which was broken into or damaged was sold to staff. This was not accounted for in the stock accounting department although the cash received from the sales was accounted for in the financial accounts. This was estimated to be no more than £2000 per annum.

Recording physical counts against the wrong lot numbers caused a considerable gain on some items and a loss on others. This was particularly so of items relating to adults' and children's clothing. The identification of wrong categories of lot numbers accounted for £15 000.

The 'cut off'

The investigation team found that a significant portion of the deficit had arisen because of inefficiencies in the company's 'cut off' procedure. The 'cut off' procedure is concerned with the arrangements made at the company's financial year end to ensure that there is agreement between physical stocks and the figures shown in the accounts, as obtained from records of purchases, sales, debtors and creditors. This procedure which should always be carefully scrutinized by both internal and external auditors is there to prevent purchases which arrive after a pre-determined date/time from being taken into stock, i.e. the cut off date/time, and vice versa for sales. Purchases which arrive after the cut off will therefore be taken into stock in the next financial year. It can be observed just how important this procedure is when one considers purchases which arrive just before a company's year end that are taken into stock. In this situation the purchases must be included in:

1   The physical stock count.
2   The book stock.
3   The purchases account.
4   The creditors figure.

It must be noted that a further difficulty that manifests itself is that it is a fact of life that there is usually a time lag between the goods arriving from suppliers and the invoice being received. This delays the matching process, e.g., Invoice with Order and Goods Received Note and could well contribute towards year end errors.

In the particular case under review there was a general 'cut off' problem which was particularly acute at the warehouse and in the area of stock accounting level. Some goods which were invoiced to the various stores were included in the physical counts. Consignments received from suppliers after the cut off date were also included in the physical counts even though there was a special cordoned off area specially reserved for goods coming in after the cut-off date.

The stock accounting department included in their GRN accruals all GRNs before the stocktake date; however, some of these consignments were not included in the physical counts. The company used merchandise delivery instructions to automatically update the purchase ledger upon origination even before the goods were sent out to the stores. Some of the delivery instructions for which goods had not been despatched by the warehouse were not taken into the stock reconciliation, neither were all the delivery instructions because some of the stamped stores copies had not been received by the warehouse for their processing and transmission for stock accounting purposes. The comptometer section had some work in progress within the cut off period. Although the married invoices, debit/credit note details were on the stock cards, nevertheless, the food delivery instructions were not posted until they were processed by the computer. Some of these delivery instructions held by the comptometer section were not taken into the stock reconciliation. The merchandise delivery instructions in particular had the effect of not only showing an anomaly between the physical counts and the stock records but also with the purchase ledger. Generally these problems were heightened by the lack of proper stocktaking instructions and procedures. These 'cut-off' problems accounted for a staggering £127 000 of the deficit.

The valuation of the findings according to causes are summarized as follows:

	£000
Falsification of accounts	40
Inconsistent pricing – price variance	30
Clerical errors	25
Errors due to denomination of quantity	119
Errors due to documentation control	107
Failure to raise correct documents	32
Incorrect stock checks	5
Wrong identification of categories	15
Error due to 'cut offs'	127
	500

The findings according to reasons have been summarized into nine categories ranging from falsification of accounts to errors due to 'cut offs'. The three major reasons were identified as contributing to approximately 70% of the deficit. The largest, errors attributed to 'cut offs', was a general problem during stocktaking and arose because of the lack of stocktaking procedures. Errors due to denomination of quantity were the second largest on the list. This was really ignorance of what quantity comprises a unit. The last major cause, errors due to documentation control, contributed to £107 000 of the deficit. Here there was no formalized standard procedure either in the area of stock accounting or at the warehouses to deal with documentation.

Falsification of accounts which represented £40 000 was attributed to stress because of the inability to balance the accounts. The errors which contributed towards the deficit contravened either the theoretical control and management of stocks or arose as a direct consequence of behavioural problems.

How did this large company get into such a mess?

As organizations grow the organizational structure and various functions must also grow and adapt to the new circumstances. Unfortunately, for a multitude of reasons, certain functions do not keep pace with the growth. In this particular case stock accounting and internal control systems relating to stocks had been neglected. However, now that management know exactly what had been going on they are now in a better position to manage and to ensure greater efficiency in the areas highlighted by the investigation.

Transfer pricing

The topic of transfer pricing provides an excellent example of how the solution to a problem requires a sophisticated understanding of objectives, circumstances, and the nature of the cost-data required.

Transfer pricing arises within a multiple profit centre form of organization. Transfer prices must be effectively managed to prevent the advantages of a multiple profit centre form of organization from being overwhelmed by the problems of inter-profit centre relationships. Transfer price information affects many critical decisions concerning the acquisition and allocation of an organization's resources, just as prices in the entire economy affect decisions concerning the allocation of a nation's wealth. Keegan and Howard (1986) said that:

> transfer pricing has assumed much importance in today's business world. Companies are repositioning themselves at a staggering pace, shedding divisions, creating or acquiring new ones, and abandoning unprofitable operations. Transfer pricing is inevitable whenever one division supplies product(s) to another.

The price at which goods (and services) are transferred between group divisions of companies can be very creative.

OBJECTIVES OF TRANSFER PRICING

Anthony and Dearden (1980) suggested that a sound transfer pricing system should accomplish the following objectives:

- It should motivate the divisional manager to make *sound decisions*, and communicate information which provides a reliable basis for such decisions.
- It should result in a report of divisional profits that is a reasonable measure of the *managerial performance* of the division.
- It should ensure that divisional *autonomy* is not undermined.

Similarly, Adelberg (1986) suggested that four interrelated criteria be used to evaluate the transfer pricing methods that could be used by profit or investment centres:

- *Goal congruence.* The transfer price that is set should send a signal to the buying and selling responsibility centres to take whatever action is in their own selfish interests and, at the same time, in the interests of the company as a whole.
- *Motivation.* It is difficult to define the internal phenomenon within an individual that 'drives' one to accomplish goals; nevertheless, the transfer price should not interfere with this process wherein the buying responsibility centre manager rationally strives to minimize his costs and the selling responsibility centre manager rationally strives to maximize his revenues.
- *Autonomy.* In a decentralized company, the managers of the buying and selling responsibility centres should be free to satisfy their own needs either internally or externally at the best possible price.
- *Performance evaluation.* Regardless of whether the buying and selling responsibility centres are cost, profit or investment centres, the transfer price should not adversely affect the 'fairness' of the performance evaluation process.

The various objectives may lead to conflict in selecting an appropriate transfer price. For example, a transfer price equal to variable cost may be appropriate to guide a short-run make-or-buy decision (objective of goal congruence), but the supplying profit centre manager may have no motivation to sell to a consuming division at variable cost because his performance measure − profit − will not be improved (objective of incentive). Moreover, if the manager of the supplier profit centre is instructed by top management to transfer at variable cost, his independence is undermined (objective of autonomy). Eccles (1985) argued that the solution to the transfer pricing problem lies not in changing transfer pricing practices but in changing other factors that influence economic decisions, or how performance is measured, evaluated, and rewarded, or both.

He went on to point out that the fundamental difficulty in managing transfer pricing involves establishing practices that will lead to decisions which enhance corporate performance, while at the same time measuring, evaluating, and rewarding performance in the light of these practices in a way that managers perceive to be fair.

In a centralized company the decision as to whether an intermediate product should be sold or processed further is determined by comparing the incremental costs of, and the revenues from, further processing. In a divisionalized organization structure, however, the manager of the receiving division will treat the price at which the intermediate product is transferred as an incremental cost, and this may lead to incorrect decisions being made.

TRANSFER PRICING 'RULES'

The literature considers the use of the 'current market price' as the transfer price, and points out its deficiencies under certain circumstances in respect of the four criteria identified above. In certain circumstances, however, the use of transfer prices based on cost-data, are deemed more appropriate.

Horngren said that there was no all-pervasive rule for transfer pricing that will lead toward an optimal economic decision. However, he suggested the following general rule would serve as a useful first step in the analysis:

> The minimum transfer price should be (a) the additional outlay costs incurred to the point of transfer (sometimes approximated by variable costs), plus (b) opportunity costs of the firm as a whole. This is the price that would ordinarily make the supplying division indifferent as to whether the output were sold inside or outside; the supplying division's contribution would be the same under either choice.

Benke and others (1982) developed a general approach to transfer pricing that shows companies how to determine a transfer price which will promote neoprofit maximization, and enhance performance evaluation. Their general rule is:

> The transfer price (TP) should equal the standard variable cost (SVC) plus the contribution margin per unit given up on the outside sale by the company when a segment sells internally. The contribution margin given up is referred to as the lost contribution margin (LCM). $TP = SVC + LCM$.

The lost contribution margin is sometimes known as the opportunity cost and is always the difference between the external market price of the intermediate product and its standard variable cost. They also said that:

> Standard cost is preferable to actual cost because of the tendency of actual cost to fluctuate and the necessity of waiting until actual prices can be determined before

transfer prices can be calculated. For responsibility centres that do not produce any products for external sale, the correct transfer price is the SVC because the LCM does not exist. However, in order to enhance performance evaluation, it is recommended to transfer the avoidable fixed costs of the product to the buying profit centre.

A pragmatic approach to the allocation/apportionment of central services expenses is described in Appendix C.

Adelberg contends that a dual transfer pricing system is necessary in light of the shortcomings of single transfer pricing systems. The buyer should use a synthetic market price equal to the variable cost of the seller plus opportunity costs to the company as a whole; and the seller should use standard full-cost plus a normal markup. Adelberg considered the use of standard costs rather than actual costs since it would leave unfavourable variances in the selling profit centre. The company as a whole will benefit from the use of standard costs because: its selling cost centres will have maximum incentive to control their costs, and its buying cost centres will no longer be unfairly penalized.

IMPLEMENTING TRANSFER PRICING

Eccles found that five major administrative process components were especially relevant to transfer pricing:

- How the transfer price is set.
- The individuals involved.
- What information is used.
- When, and under what conditions, are transfer prices set or charged.
- How conflict is managed.

He also found that although there was a relationship between policy and the nature of the administrative process used to implement it, a great deal of variation was possible. He found that the administrative process was also affected by other aspects of a company's strategy, e.g. by technological and market characteristics of the transferred product and the products that incorporate it, and by general business conditions.

THE USE OF COST-DATA

When a policy of 'mandated full-cost (i.e. absorption cost)' transfers is used, the transfer pricing problem becomes one of measuring the cost of production for the intermediate good. There are two principal ways for establishing the mandated full-cost: 'actual cost' of production, and the 'standard cost' i.e. what it should cost. Between these two measures is a range of possibilities defined by who pays for any difference between what it should have cost to make, and the actual cost.

Variances from standard costs can be caused by actions and outcomes of both buying and selling profit centres. Although standard full-cost transfer prices insulate buying centres from events that affect the performance of the selling profit centres and other buying profit centres, they do not insulate selling profit centres from events that affect the performance of buying profit centres. As a result, variances are reported in the selling profit centre, and they affect both its performance as a cost centre on internal sales and its performance as a profit centre on external sales.

Although in theory, the three types of variances (volume, efficiency, and purchasing) can be separated in terms of which profit centre is responsible for them, in practice there is always some ambiguity. The selling profit centre does not have much influence on the volume, or order sizes etc. of internal sales. These may lead to manufacturing inefficiencies in the selling profit centre. There is further ambiguity regarding whether the standard costs are 'what they should be'.

In practice, surveys by Tomkins (1973) and Rook (1971) indicate that many firms use cost-plus transfer prices when there is no market for the intermediate product. There is a danger that cost-plus based transfer prices will motivate the manager of the receiving division to restrict output below that of the optimal output level for the company as a whole.

Eccles concludes that:

> No system is perfect. When standard cost transfer prices are used, disputes about who is responsible for variances and the existence of gaming behaviour reflect the fact that there are no definitive answers to the questions of what 'true' standard costs are and how much of the capacity in the selling profit centre buyers should be held responsible for.

and that:

> The underlying difficulty in determining actual costs is that some judgement must be exercised about such issues as joint and by-product cost allocations. The underlying difficulty in determining standard costs is that some judgement must be exercised in making the assumptions that become the basis of calculating these standards. For both of these difficulties, *there are no purely technical solutions that will be accepted by all parties involved.*

Typically, conflict is a result of three major and closely related causes:

- Lack of strategic clarity.
- Performance measurement, evaluation, and reward criteria that emphasize individual profit centre financial results.
- Inadequacies in the process by which transfer prices are determined.

Each of these factors must be addressed in the context of the others. Resolving these conflicts requires a willingness on the part of the profit centre managers involved to reach an agreement.

On the international scene the price at which goods and services are transferred can be greatly affected by the taxation systems of the countries involved.

It must be remembered that transfer pricing can cause certain companies within a group or certain divisions within an organization to look as though they are performing better or worse than they really are!

Summary

Creativity in the area of stock valuation encompasses much of what has already been described in relation to the elements of cost, i.e. materials, labour, direct expenses and overheads. Yes, stock valuation may be subjected to quadruple creativity and more!

The Statement of Standard Accounting Practices 9 (SSAP 9) and the Companies

Act 1985 provide general rules, guidance and much food for thought about the amount at which stocks are to be stated in the accounts of companies. It is a fact that SSAP 9 actually recognizes and states that 'the valuation of stock is subject to wide differences and variations.'

The wording of the SSAP 9 also promotes creativity because it is subject to differing interpretations, e.g. 'fairest practical approximation'; 'reasonable relationship to the actual cost obtained'; 'actual costs should exclude abnormal conversion costs'; 'foreseeable losses' and so on.

Creativity in the stock valuation area tends to manifest itself in:

- Cost definition problems: the treatment of transport, handling costs, rebates, conversion costs and overheads may all have a dramatic impact upon the figures produced.
- The calculation of the net realizable value: decisions have to be taken about the way in which selling, distribution and manufacturing expenses are to be incorporated.
- The grouping of stock items.

LONG TERM CONTRACTS

In addition to ascertaining the appropriate amounts for materials, labour and over-heads applicable to long term contracts, there are other creative factors which include:

1 The treatment of stocks of materials and plant and machinery, on site and returned from site.
2 The ascertainment of foreseeable losses/outcomes.
3 Conservatism re the amount of profit to be taken on uncompleted and completed contracts, i.e. because of uncertainty/possible additional work in the future which has to be paid for by the contractor.

MINI CASES

The first mini case was included in this chapter to help make the point that errors can be creative.

The second case illustrates that given pretty identical circumstances relating to plant, there can be wide variations between the figures that are produced.

THE CASE OF THE HALF-MILLION POUNDS STOCK DEFICIT

This was a real life story of an investigation into the reasons for a half-million pounds stock deficit. It highlights the fact that a disorganized stock-take can be extremely creative! The principal causes of the variance were the result of errors in the denomination of quantity, documentation control and cut-off procedure.

As an organization grows the cost accounting function needs to keep pace with the growth. To ignore this aspect is to invite creativity via errors and the late arrival of control information.

TRANSFER PRICING

It is inevitable when one division or company within a group supplies goods to another division/group member that transfer pricing is utilized.

It is a subject which is far too wide to be covered in great depth in this book. However, many authors have written on the subject and provide evidence that here is quite a complex and creative area. Transfer pricing can be particularly creative when used on an international basis by multi-national companies.

Where transfer pricing is involved it may be very difficult to assess divisional performance fairly.

A repeat

Remember that the area of stock valuation is subject to *wide differences and variations!*

Part 3

Costing methods

8
Absorption costing

We repeat, and cannot stress enough that the treatment of overheads:
- Is an area in which, perhaps, there is the greatest scope for creativity.
- Does have a dramatic impact upon the costs which are assigned to cost centres, goods and services.

With absorption (total or full) costing there is greater subjectivity (i.e. personal judgements) than there is with marginal costing. This is because in absorption costing many of the so-called fixed overheads are absorbed by production via the absorption costing system. Greater subjectivity leads to greater creativity!

This chapter attempts to look critically at absorption costing (including the treatment of service departments) and in so doing hopes to highlight the creative aspects.

Great care should be exercised when using absorption costing to formulate selling prices. The treatment of overheads could mean the loss of a contract. Product pricing is covered in more depth in Chapter 14.

Absorption costing – a critical view

Decisions may be made which totally ignore the limitations of absorption costing!

The members of the board of directors studied carefully the figures produced for them by the accountant. After some discussion had taken place, the finance director concluded, 'Product X is making a substantial loss, I therefore propose that we discontinue its production'. The proposal was eagerly seconded by the production director and received unanimous support. The figures considered by the directors had been prepared using absorption costing!

Were the directors right to discontinue the production of Product X?

Is absorption costing really an appropriate method for this type of decision making?

Were the directors aware of the limitations of the information on which they based their decision?

Unless you have a single product environment, such a bold statement is difficult to justify. To my mind it is pretty near impossible to end up with a reliable product profit or loss with an absorption costing system. Absorption costing systems were really designed to ensure that all costs were covered. They were not designed to give accurate product costs.

Fig. 8.1 and the following notes attempt to explain how absorption costing systems work and their limitations.

Notes

STEP 1. The overheads, in terms of indirect materials, labour and expenses have to be estimated well before the new accounting period commences. This will take into account past performance, future production and sales, inflation and environmental perceptions, etc.

LIMITATION 1. Thus, right from the word go, the fact that figures have to be pre-determined brings subjectivity into play. The accountant and the management should always remember that the overheads being absorbed are only *estimates*! If they are way out, the whole system falls flat at the first hurdle. Hence, the need to monitor and to ensure that rates are revised to take account of changes in basic assumptions, etc.

STEP 2. Overheads which can be identified with a particular cost centre are charged direct to the cost centre concerned, i.e. *allocated.*
  Examples of allocated costs are:
- The wages of a cleaner employed solely in the assembly department will be allocated to the assembly department.
- A special cleaning fluid used only in the paint department will be allocated to the paint department.

LIMITATION 2. In absorption costing the allocation process poses the least problems. However, it must still be remembered that the overheads being allocated *are still only estimates*. The allocation process is assisted by the analysis of time sheets/clock cards for indirect labour and material issue notes for indirect materials updated by future plans. It must be remembered, however, that the time sheets/clock cards and material issue notes represent historic data. Circumstances may change, e.g. the cleaner who was expected to clean only in one department may clean up in two departments. Yes, allocation does rely upon a number of perceived assumptions! If identification with a particular cost centre cannot be resolved then the overheads in question will have to be apportioned.

STEP 3. Overheads which cannot be identified with a particular cost centre are apportioned using some arbitrary basis, e.g.

Item	*Method of apportionment*
Insurance of buildings Depreciation of buildings }	Floor area occupied or cubic capacity occupied
Welfare services Canteen }	In proportion to the number of employees

The accountant will select the basis which he/she considers to be the most appropriate and will also have to rely upon technical estimates for apportioning certain overhead expenditure.

LIMITATION 3. The bases which are used to apportion overheads to cost centres are subjective. The selection of the basis usually rests with the accountant. Accountants are people, and as such are very complex variables! No two accountants will ever think alike! Accountants will continue to select different bases of apportionment for the same types of cost within the same industry!

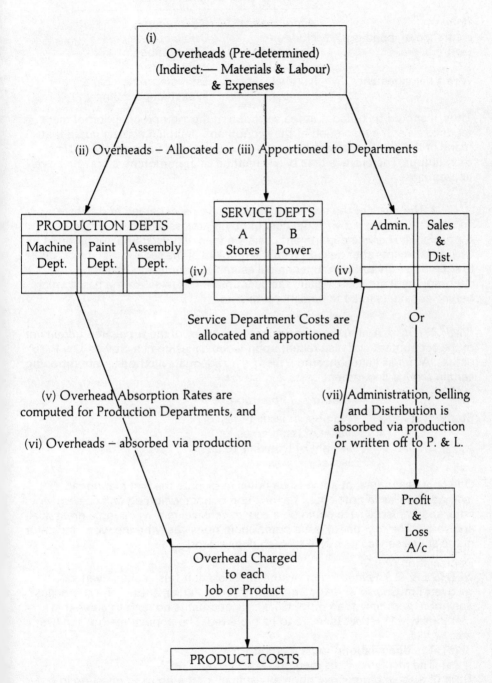

Fig 8.1   *The absorption of overheads*

For example

Item	Accountant Y	Accountant Z
Insurance of buildings	Floor area	Cubic capacity
Lighting	Floor area	The number of kilo-watt hours
Works management	Number of employees	Estimated time spent in each department

Thus, it should be noted that the selection of the method of apportionment tends to be at the discretion of the accountant. It should also be noted that many of the overheads which have to be apportioned vary more with time than output. Therefore, a time based method of apportionment may be more appropriate.

STEP 4. The costs of the service departments are ascertained and, where appropriate, compared with the cost of buying the service from outside suppliers. The service department costs are then allocated and apportioned to user departments after dealing with the problem of the service that they provide to each other. In addition to technical estimates various methods of apportionment are used. Again, the accountant has to select the basis which he/she considers to be the most appropriate.

LIMITATION 4. Again, the outcome is at the mercy of the subjective judgement of the accountant and also reliant upon technical estimates provided by third parties. As far as I am concerned, there is no adequate method for apportioning certain service department costs, e.g. stores.

Item	Method of apportionment
Stores cost	Number of issue notes, or value of issue notes, or weight of materials to be issued

One only has to look at a few issue notes to dispute the first mentioned method. One issue note could be for a component weighing and costing very little, another issue note could be a very expensive item weighing a great deal, and so on. The number of issue notes could quite easily be the worst indicator of the stores service provided to each department!

STEPS 5 & 6. The method of overhead absorption (also called overhead recovery) must also be selected. As mentioned earlier, a lot of the overheads vary more with time than output. Thus, accountants do tend to agree that methods which reflect time are to be preferred. The popular methods in use are:
  (a) The direct labour hours method.
  (b) The machine hours method.
Both of these methods rely upon an estimate of the hours in question in order to work out the absorption rate. The rates are calculated as follows:

$$\text{Direct labour hour rate} = \frac{\text{Overheads for the cost centre}}{\text{Estimated number of direct labour hours for the cost centre}}$$

68

$$\text{Machine hour rate} = \frac{\text{Overheads for the cost centre}}{\text{Estimated number of machine hours for the cost centre}}$$

As production flows through the cost centres, these overhead absorption rates are applied in an attempt to recover the overheads, e.g. if the direct labour hour rate for the assembly department is £24 per direct labour hour, and job X9L5007 spends 3.5 hours in that department, the overheads charged to the job (i.e. recovered) will be:

$$3.5 \times £24 = \underline{£84}$$

This system relies on an efficient system of time recording.

LIMITATIONS 5 & 6. The limitations corresponding to steps 5 and 6 are pretty obvious. The selection of the method of overhead absorption rests with the accountant. In addition to the two methods described above there are other methods which may be adopted, e.g. percentage of prime cost; percentage of wages, etc. The numerator in the calculation suffers from all of the drawbacks which have been pointed out in relation to steps 1 to 4 inclusive, in one word, subjectivity. The denominator depends upon the accuracy of predicting the future level of activity. The denominator, e.g. direct labour hours or machine hours, is *only an estimate*. This is why the end product tends to be an under or over-absorption of overheads! Stock valuations computed using the absorption costing principle tend to be unaffected by the accounting treatment of the under or over-absorption, the under or over-absorption, being dealt with in the Profit and Loss Account. The following example should illustrate the point which I am trying to make:

Absorption Costing
Trading and Profit and Loss Account

		£	£	£
Sales 5700 Units @ £10 each				57 000
less Cost of sales:				
Opening stock	500 units @ £5		2 500	
add Production costs				
Materials	6000 units @ £2	12 000		
Labour	6000 units @ £3	18 000		
Overheads	6000 units @ £2	12 000	42 000	
	$\overline{7}$		44 500	
*less Closing stock (FIFO)***				
	800 units @ £7		5 600	38 900
Gross Profit				18 100
less Administration, selling and distributive costs				9 400
				8 700
*less *Over-absorption of overhead*				2 000
Net Profit				£6 700

In this particular case the stock valuation is over-stated by some of the over-absorbed overheads! Why not simply treat the under/over absorption as an adjustment to the current period's production costs?

*   The actual overheads amounted to £10 000.

**   FIFO – The First In, First Out method of stock valuation was used in the above example. There are quite a number of other methods which could have been used in its place. Yet more subjectivity!

In addition, problems could also be encountered via the time recording systems, e.g. incorrect recording/behavioural factors.

STEP 7. A decision has to be taken as to how much, if any, of the administration selling and distribution expenses are to be included in product costs. Companies do include varying combinations of those costs in their product costs. The accountant has to decide how such costs will be shared out between the various products/jobs. Not an easy task. In some companies all or some of the costs are simply written off in the Profit and Loss Account.

LIMITATION 7. The division of administration, selling and distribution costs between products/jobs is an extremely difficult task. The accountant is faced yet again with the problem of selecting an appropriate method, e.g. percentage on prime cost. One rule of thumb method which I myself have come across was 50% of prime cost to recover administration costs – not very scientific! The accountant has also to sort out which costs, if any, will be written off to the Profit and Loss Account.

GREY AREAS

In some cases certain overhead expenditure finds its way into a product cost when in fact that expenditure had nothing at all to do with the particular product concerned. This has happened with Research and Development expenditure (R & D). Products which have received no benefit whatsoever from R & D have had to bear a share of the R & D costs, the result being to understate their profits and overstate the profits on the product/s which did in fact benefit from the R & D.

If you ask around, you will hear of lots of complaints via subsidiary companies and departments within companies that they are being charged for services/administration on a very unjust basis!

As stated, time and time again throughout this book, the application of absorption costing depends upon the accuracy of the estimates and upon the subjective judgement of the accountant.

A lot of qualified accountants who move into industry have very little industrial experience. Quite a substantial number of these accountants are really financial accountants. Yet, many of them are called upon to become involved in absorption costing systems. With many of them, their only encounter with absorption costing has been study courses, textbooks and their examinations. On finding out that they are now expected to become involved with absorption costing they run very quickly to textbooks and their old study notes. One has only to look at the past exam questions set by the various professional bodies in the subject to realize that they may in fact have been guilty of introducing misconceptions. Here are just a few examples:

Item	Method of apportionment
Depreciation of plant and machinery	Plant valuation
Indirect labour	Direct labour hours
Consumable stores	Direct labour hours

Depreciation can be split up far more accurately than the method stated. Companies keep plant registers, they know the locations of their plant and equipment and it is possible to calculate the depreciation per department/cost centre with accuracy.

In the case of indirect labour the employees concerned are quite capable of recording their time spent in each department/cost centre via time sheets, etc. This historic information would form a sound starting point for assessing the indirect labour cost per department/cost centre for the forthcoming accounting period.

Records will be kept of the consumable stores used per department/cost centre and these should form the basis of estimating the consumable stores usage per department/cost centre in the next accounting period.

Thus, quite a number of items can be shared out using far more realistic methods than some of those used in textbooks/examination questions. Companies do keep records of indirect labour, indirect materials and depreciation on a departmental/cost centre basis. Therefore, accountants who have to use absorption costing should aim to use the practical common sense methods based upon an analysis of their company's own data.

It should be noted that there are many variations to the steps/methods described in relation to the diagram (Fig. 8.1). It is really up to each company to tailor the system to meet their needs.

As indicated, there is a real need to monitor the system on a regular basis and adjust the absorption rates for changes in basic assumptions, e.g. inflation, levels of activity, etc.

Warning! Please don't expect too much from an absorption costing system, especially in terms of assessing product profitability.

Service department costs – a critical view

The ascertainment, allocation and apportionment of service department costs is a veritable mine field!

Numerous cost and management accounting texts recommend a wide assortment of methods for the apportionment of service department costs.

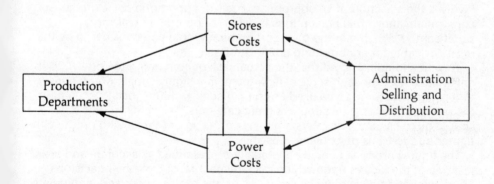

Fig 8.2   *Service department costs*

Quite a number of the methods described in texts or used in examination questions are, to my mind, most unsuitable for real life situations. Thus, in an absorption costing system the treatment of service costs is really a jungle of subjectivity and imprecision.

Why attempt to compute service department costs? The aims are twofold:
1   To ascertain the cost of providing a service and where practicable to make

comparisons with the cost of buying the service from outside suppliers, and

2   To be in a position to charge user departments for their usage of the service.

Pre-determined overheads have to be allocated and apportioned to service department cost centres. Thus, from the outset it must be remembered that all the costs being dealt with are estimates. Their accuracy depends upon a number of variables and perceived assumptions. It is quite likely that the estimates will never match the actual expenditure. Those overheads which can be identified with specific service departments can be allocated to the departments concerned. Those overheads which cannot be identified with particular departments have to be apportioned using an arbitrary basis. The personnel responsible for the apportionment of overheads to service departments have to select and apply the basis of apportionment which they consider to be the most appropriate for each type of expense. The selection of an appropriate basis of apportionment is, therefore, dependent upon subjective judgement. Decision making in the area of apportionment does involve consideration of a number of alternatives, e.g. floor area versus cubic capacity; number of employees versus number of direct labour hours. The way in which costs are apportioned can, in fact, be quite creative! The method used could help to indicate, for example, that it is more economical to provide a particular service when compared with buying the service from outside sources, or vice versa!

Another problem is caused because in addition to serving production, administration, selling and distribution departments, many service departments also serve each other. The treatment of services provided to/from other service departments brings materiality into play. If the amounts in question are insignificant or tend to cancel each other out, then it would appear to be quite an acceptable practice to simply ignore such items.

Service departments usually benefit to some extent from the administrative function. It is extremely difficult to decide how much (if any!) of the administrative costs should be charged to service departments. The task involves the selection of an appropriate basis of apportionment. What is appropriate? Individual perceptions of what is appropriate will vary significantly! Which method of apportionment would you consider to be the most equitable for apportioning administration costs?

Thus, it should be noted that the actual task of computing the pre-determined cost for each service department is a highly subjective matter. Where such costs are to be used as comparisons with the costs of obtaining the services from outside suppliers great care must be exercised. The aim should be to eliminate any personal bias on the part of those who produce the figures and to be as objective as possible.

The figures produced could never really be described as accurate and are just one of the factors upon which management must base their decisions. Management do have to make decisions on the basis of poor and incomplete information, e.g. the estimated costs of a particular service department and the fact that a lot of the costs assigned to it cannot be identified with it!

In its favour, one can say that an attempt to asertain the costs of service departments is better than no attempt.

Some of the methods of apportioning service department costs to user departments are described and discussed below and are as follows:

1   *Ignoring the service that they provide each other*. This method is appropriate in cases where the services provided to each other tend to compensate and

cancel each other out, or the amounts in question are insignificant.

In the real world it is unlikely that the services provided to fellow service departments will in fact compensate and cancel out. The application of the materiality concept to a costing environment is highly subjective. What is significant for one company may be regarded as insignificant by another company in the same industry and of a similar size!

2 *Set order of clearing* (two steps or specified order of clearing). In this method service departments are apportioned in a specific order. Once the service has been apportioned it does not receive an apportionment of costs from the service departments which are apportioned after it.

The specific order has to be determined, e.g. the first to be apportioned being the service department which receives least benefit from the other service departments.

The order in which they are cleared does therefore depend upon the subjective judgement of the accountant/personnel involved. The method ignores the use of services by service departments already cleared from those not yet cleared (see Fig. 8.3).

	Service departments			Production departments		
£'000	Power	Stores	Welfare	A	B	C
Overheads	60	100	30	720	640	830
Power	−60	5	2	20	20	13
		105				
Stores		−105	3	38	42	22
			35			
Welfare			−35	15	10	10
				793	712	875

Fig 8.3   The set order of clearing method

Whoever decided upon the order of clearing in Fig. 8.3 decided that the order would be: first, power; second, stores and last, welfare. Any use of stores and welfare by power is ignored in this example. Also any use of welfare by power and stores is ignored. Another problem encountered is the answer to the question, which methods of apportionment should be used to share up the power, the stores and the welfare between user departments (excluding service departments already cleared)?

3 *Repeated distribution* (or continuous allotment). The order in which the service departments are to be apportioned must still be established. This method does take into account the services provided by service departments to each other. When the cost of a service department has been apportioned and cleared it may then receive a cost apportionment/s from other service departments which have to be re-apportioned. This task repeats itself until all service departments have a nil balance. This method is perhaps best illustrated by the following example (Fig. 8.4).

	Service departments		Production departments	
	Stores £	Maintenance £	A £	Z £
Amounts allocated and apportioned	24 000	45 000	113 000	63 000
Stores (shared 1:5:2)	−24 000	3 000	15 000	6 000
		48 000		
Maintenance (shared 1:8:3)	4 000	−48 000	32 000	12 000
Stores (shared 1:5:2)	−4 000	500	2 500	1 000
Maintenance (shared 1:8:3)	42	−500	333	125
Stores (shared 1:5:2)	−42	5	26	11
Maintenance (shared 1:8:3)		−5	4	7
			£162 863	£82 137

Fig 8.4 The repeated distribution method

It can be observed that having ascertained the amount allocated and apportioned to each service and production department, the stores cost is split up between the other three departments in the ratio of 1:5:2 respectively and the maintenance cost is split up between the other three departments in the ratio of 1:8:3 respectively. How laborious! The method does give a perception of accuracy which could lead to unfortunate decisions, e.g. closing down a department because of the ways in which the absorption costing system computed the figures. The aim of absorption costing is simply to ensure that all costs are covered. It is impossible for absorption costing systems to provide accurate service and production department costs. So, why spend a lot of time and effort using methods such as repeated distribution etc. for dealing with the apportionment of service department costs? Surely, there must be a better way.

4 *Simultaneous equations.* The simultaneous equation method is rather cumbersome and is not really suitable for situations involving more than two service departments. The reason for this is that each additional service department creates yet another 'unknown'.

5 *Technical estimates.* This is perhaps the best method for apportioning service department costs. However, it is still an estimate and dependent upon the ability of the estimator.

6 *Transfer pricing.* The difficulty with transfer pricing is the transfer price! It is very difficult to fix equitable transfer prices. Behavioural factors may lead to charging for certain services at a profit!

7 *Bases devised to apportion specific department costs.*
Power: in the good old days one method advocated was lbs of steam. Nowadays the bases tend to be floor area or cubic capacity or kilowatt hours or technical estimates or number of radiators (for heating) or number of power points.
  It is clear from the above that there is quite a wide choice. It is also clear

that a choice has to be made. Which basis is the most appropriate? There is no easy answer to this question. In certain user departments floor area may be more important than cubic capacity or vice versa, yet a choice of one basis only has to be made. Some of the other methods mentioned are quite dubious, e.g. the number of radiators or plug points could give a misleading indication of power consumption. However, it should be noted that the most accurate method is metered consumption per department. With the advances in electronics and the use of 'chips' metered consumption ought to be more and more practicable.

In the absence of metered consumption, I believe that the most appropriate basis for apportioning the power service department costs to user departments is to use technical estimates of consumption per department. Having said that, it must be remembered that to estimate the consumption per department with accuracy is quite an undertaking. Consumption will be affected by short-time, overtime, shift work, the disposal and/or acquisition of new machines, the weather, production levels, stock levels, sales levels, cancelled orders, etc.

Personnel: texts suggest that this can be split up between departments according to the number of employees or wages paid. These methods may not satisfactorily reflect the amount of work per department carried out by the personnel department. Maybe, a method based upon the rate of labour turnover per department may be more appropriate! Computers should make it possible for a more detailed breakdown of personnel department costs per user department. I would suggest that personnel costs be divided up between those which can be identified with a particular department e.g. advertising, interviewing time and those which cannot, e.g. light and heat of the personnel department offices. Those which could be identified with a particular department/location (i.e. cost centre) could be charged direct to the cost centre concerned. Those which could not be identified with user departments would have to be apportioned. Because many of these remaining costs tend to be time based, maybe a time based method such as direct labour hours is the most appropriate. This does involve personal perceptions and personal judgements.

Maintenance: technical estimates based on past performance and future expectations tend to be recommended and used. The problem here is that, except for the routine maintenance of fixed assets, it is difficult to predict the unexpected and account for uncertainty. The weather can have a dramatic impact upon the level of building maintenance. The skill of employees can lead to increased/decreased levels of maintenance work on machinery and plant.

Stores: to my mind, this is possibly the most difficult of all. I cannot see that any method will yield meaningful results. Methods put forward for apportioning the stores cost to user departments are:
(a) The value of material issued.
(b) The value of material stored.
(c) The cubic capacity of material handled.
(d) The number of requisitions (i.e. issue notes).
(e) The weight of material handled.
Which is the most equitable method for dealing with the stores cost? I would suggest that none of these is really suitable as the stores function consists of a number of variables. The above methods all use a single

variable and method (d) is quite suspect. Here again, computers could be used in an attempt to make a more meaningful evaluation. The stores cost could be divided up into different component parts, e.g. those costs which could be charged to user departments via an analysis of stores' personnel time sheets (yes, store keepers can still keep records of how they spend their time); secondly, those costs which could be charged to user departments on a cubic capacity basis, e.g. the costs of managing the space occupied – light, heat, etc.; thirdly, those costs connected with the value of the stock, e.g. insurance of stocks; finally, those costs which could be split up according to their weight. Another alternative would be to devise a formula which takes a number of variables into account. The quest for greater accuracy does lead one to ask, is it all worth it? Why go to all this trouble when the resulting figures can never be classed as accurate? It is also raises the cost/benefit question.

What can be done?
If service department costs have to be ascertained and charged to user departments then a common sense approach to the problem is essential. I would suggest that the following approach could be adopted:

1 Allocate and apportion the pre-determined costs using the most equitable basis. Thus, we cannot avoid subjectivity, even at the outset. Costs have to be estimated, bases of apportionment must be selected. Remember however, that the payroll analysis for direct and indirect labour, the materials usage analysis, the machine utilization information may help with the quest to provide more realistic bases of apportionment.
2 Deal with inter-service transfers. To my mind the services provided by service departments to fellow service departments should be dealt with before any apportionment is made to production departments. This should ensure that the service department costs are more realistic, e.g. amounts allocated and apportioned to the service department plus the cost of other services used by that service department less the cost of services provided to other service departments. A simple illustration of this principle in action is the case where the driver of the internal transport was given a medical check organized by the welfare department. Internal transport should be charged with the cost of the medical, thus their costs increase. Welfare costs should be reduced by the amount of the medical. A simple system of debits and credits!
3 Deal with any service department costs which can be allocated to a particular cost centre. Examples of allocatable service department costs are:
   (a) Maintenance work to be carried out for a particular department.
   (b) Routine maintenance per department.
   (c) Welfare expenditure which can be identified with a particular department.
4 Divide the remainder of the service departments' costs up into groups, e.g.
   (a) Those costs which vary with time.
   (b) Those costs which vary with space.
   (c) Those costs which vary with the number of employees, and so on.
As was mentioned in relation to the apportionment of stores costs the costs which have to be apportioned should not be grouped together and apportioned using just a single variable. A combination along the lines suggested above should lead to a more realistic apportionment.

Why go to all that trouble? Yesteryear, maybe it would have been going too

76

far. Nowadays, with the aid of computers, it should be possible to make more realistic apportionments of service department costs.

Both textbooks and the examination questions of professional bodies propagate the idea that certain methods of apportionment are acceptable. In fact, they tend to give such methods a degree of respectability and a perceived sense of accuracy. Here are a few examples:

One method which has been frequently used/suggested for apportioning stores costs is the number of requisitions (i.e. issue notes). One issue note may be for a very small item weighing a few grams and costing 50p, another issue note could be for a very heavy/bulky item costing £2500. Thus, the method takes no account of size, weight or value. As mentioned earlier, possibly the best solution is to use a number of methods for apportioning the stores costs.

One method for apportioning depreciation of machinery/equipment to cost centres (including service departments) is to share it between them in proportion to the value of machinery/equipment. This method ignores the life of the asset and the estimated residual value, if any. However, depreciation of machinery/equipment in a lot of cases is a cost which can be *allocated*, i.e. identified with a department and charged direct to the department concerned.

Indirect wages may be apportioned using a variety of methods. Yet, here also it should be possible to allocate it direct to the user departments. Time recording and analysis also takes place re indirect labour, e.g. time sheets, clock cards etc. The indirect labour force are quite capable of recording how and where they spend their time! This does and should happen in practice, so why have textbook writers/examiners past and present continued to ignore this fact of life?

The danger of the above is that certain accountants, e.g. those trained in a financial accounting environment that move to a cost accounting environment, may, without any thought whatsoever, adopt one/some of these dubious methods.

Following on from the dubious methods of apportionment it must be stressed that those who are responsible for this activity must make better use of:

1 The payroll analysis for direct and indirect labour.
2 The materials analysis.
3 The machine utilization analysis.
4 The plant register/fixed asset schedules/capital expenditure budgets.

This historic data should provide a firm foundation upon which to compute the pre-determined overheads for the forthcoming period. It should also provide a more accurate method of allocating and apportioning overheads to cost centres and service department costs to fellow service departments and other user departments.

Technology has moved forward for many years with great speed. To some extent the area of cost/service department apportionments has remained relatively static. Cost accountants have failed in a lot of cases to latch onto and harness new technology in their quest for greater accuracy.
Meters/measuring devices are available for a multiplicity of purposes and at a cost which may be afforded. What was impossible some years ago is now possible because of advances in technology. The computer can generate all kinds of information, information which several years ago would just not have been available.

More work is needed in this area to develop more sophisticated methods and more meaningful results.

Warning! Although I have striven to provide a more common sense approach it must be remembered that the apportionment of pre-determined figures can never be classed as accurate. One must not lose sight of the aim of absorption costing, i.e. an attempt to ensure that all costs are covered. Hence its other name, total costing.

Summary

The bulk of this chapter was provided by the reproduction of two of Leslie Chadwick's journal articles.

Management, and indeed many accountants, fail to appreciate the limitations of absorption costing. This is why absorption costing tends to be used in areas for which it was not really designed, e.g. decision making. It is simply an attempt to ensure that all costs are covered. The failure to ignore the limitations is, in our opinion, the reason for 'innocent creativity', i.e. those involved are unaware that they have been creative!

Cost and management accounting texts and examiners may also be guilty of promoting innocent creativity. They may advocate or use methods which are inappropriate to a real world environment, e.g. methods of apportionment such as the value of machinery, etc. when more practical and realistic methods are available. There is a possibility that inexperienced accountants/accounting staff and even experienced accountants may adopt some of these inappropriate methods!

Creativity in the absorption costing area exists in profusion because:

- The overheads have to be pre-determined on the basis of past performance and future expectations. Perceptions about the environment in which the organization operates involve numerous judgements. Judgements made by the cost and management function. It is very difficult to predict the future with accuracy. Past performance is not always a good indication of what will happen in the future.

- The process of cost allocation also depends upon perceptions and assumptions about the future, e.g. how and where indirect workers are to spend their time.

- There are many bases of apportionment, e.g. floor area, cubic capacity, number of employees, from which a selection has to be made.

- Quite a lot of space was devoted to the critical review of service department costs. The comments which were made above also apply to service department costing. However, with service departments there are a number of other problems. Creativity may arise as a result of the way in which service cost centres are apportioned between themselves and other cost centres. The service provided to each other may simply be ignored on the grounds of materiality or incorporated via the various other methods in a number of different ways. The methods by which service cost centres' costs are to be apportioned have to be selected. The computations involved may, in fact, give a perceived false sense of accuracy!

  Certain services, e.g. stores are extremely difficult to apportion fairly. It would appear that there is a need for new thinking and perhaps a multi-variable approach to the problem is worthy of serious consideration. Costs can never be accurate, but they can be more accurate!

- Absorption rates must also be selected and a variety of methods are available, e.g. direct labour hour rates, machine hour rates, etc. The denominator used in the calculation must also be estimated, e.g. the direct labour hours, machine hours, etc. for the period concerned.

- Absorption costing breeds under and over absorption caused by variations between actual overheads/level of activity incurred and the pre-determined overheads/level of activity. A recommended method of dealing with the under/over absorption is to include it in the Profit and Loss Account. This treatment means that the stocks of finished goods and work-in-progress are either under or overstated! The fact that under/over absorption exists highlights and advertises the inaccuracy of absorption costing.
- Decisions have to be made re the treatment of administration, selling and distribution expenses. They can be written off to the Profit and Loss Account or absorbed in the cost of products and/or services produced. Various combinations can be found in practice. Their treatment could spark off a certain amount of conflict!
- Examples can be found of costs apportioned to cost centres/products which neither directly nor indirectly benefit from the particular cost, e.g. R & D for a new product development.

The mini-examples described in this chapter illustrate that: the treatment of R & D could lead companies into discontinuing the production of profitable products; the absorption costing system could bring about the cessation of production of a product or the closure of a department or a factory; it is impossible in a number of cases to find a realistic method of apportionment, e.g. stores cost; organizations need to make more use of their own data, e.g. payroll analysis re indirect workers; the treatment of administrative overheads can lead to conflict in both private and public sector organizations; examiners and textbook writers can promote unsound methods; there are many many decisions which have to be made using subjective judgement.

There is a great need for more research in the area of absorption costing and the development of multi-variable computer packages for the apportionment of overheads (including service department costs). The technology is now available to provide absorption costing with a more sophisticated approach to the age old problem of dealing with overheads.

The environment in which organizations operate is one of frequent change. Monitoring therefore, on a regular basis, is a prerequisite to the working of an efficient costing system. Changes in the basic assumptions about the future may render all/most of the pre-determined overheads, anticipated levels of activity meaningless. Meaningless information is of little value to the company, but if it is not amended or replaced and continues to be used it will no doubt be very creative!

A repeat

Absorption costing simply attempts to ensure that all costs are covered.

9

Marginal costing*

Period III	Product £000	Product £000	Product £000	Total £000
Sales	120	90	340	550
less variable cost (i.e. marginal cost)	60	60	190	310
Contribution	60	30	150	240
less fixed costs				110
PROFIT =				130

Marginal costing treats fixed costs as period costs i.e. they are written off in the period in which they are incurred and are not therefore included in stock valuations. In the above example the total fixed costs for the period, £110 000, were deducted from the total of all the contributions made by each product.

On occasions, examination questions and texts have tended to mislead their readers by apportioning the fixed costs between products. This is not marginal costing. However, it is quite a dangerous practice. It is very difficult to find a method which will apportion the fixed costs between products which is fair. How many businesses have dropped a particular product on the basis of such unsound information?

The following article describes the creative aspects of marginal costing and breakeven analysis.

Marginal costing – a critical view

Beware of over-simplifications; marginal costing needs to be applied with care.

It has already been pointed out that many overheads varied more with time than output and also that certain overheads could not be identified with a department/cost centre. Marginal costing attempts to overcome these problems. Marginal costing is really all about five areas:

1 Cost behaviour.
2 The relationship between sales revenue, variable costs and the contribution.

* Marginal Costing is also known as Direct Costing or Variable Costing

3   The treatment of fixed costs.
4   Changes in the volume or the type of output.
5   Break-even analysis.

However, marginal costing theory tends to be so over-simplified that its adoption could lead unsuspecting managerial teams into making decisions which go wrong. It should be noted at the outset that marginal costing is really a technique designed for use in the short-term.

COST BEHAVIOUR

The marginal costing system depends upon being able to divide costs between variable costs (i.e. marginal costs) and fixed costs.

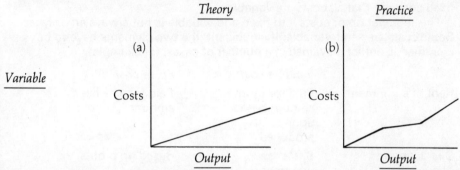

Variable costs – 'Vary with the level of activity, (e.g. direct materials and direct labour) within a relevant range.'

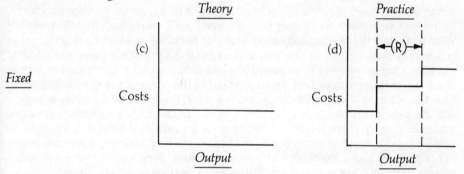

Fixed costs – 'Those which remain unchanged irrespective of the level of activity (e.g. rates, rent, salaries) within a relevant range (R).'

The variable cost per unit will not always be a uniform amount as depicted by the theoretical position disclosed in (a) above. At certain levels of activity costs will fluctuate, e.g. direct materials may become less expensive, direct labour may become more expensive and vice versa (see (b) above). The assumption that the last unit produced will have the same variable cost as the first unit produced does not hold good in the real world of business. Variable costs are affected by changes in the environment, internal, e.g. strikes, production efficiency etc. and external, e.g. political, social and economic factors, technological change, developments in product and factor markets. If production departments have to meet specific delivery dates for certain customers this will no doubt affect variable costs, e.g. the acquisition costs of key components purchased in small quantities and overtime worked to ensure completion by the delivery date.

Fixed costs do not remain unchanged irrespective of the level of activity as portrayed in (c). A fairer reflection of what really happens with fixed costs is shown in (d). In the real world, even in the short-term, there could well be 'step fixed costs'. Management could be guilty of going overboard on theory! They assume that if they increase output, their fixed costs will remain unchanged. Unfortunately for them, this does not always happen; fixed costs increase and profits go down. Fixed costs may move up or down. More plant, machinery, equipment and property will increase fixed costs but such assets can also be disposed of and therefore reduce fixed costs. Spare capacity in terms of equipment and space may even be sub-let. This would also reduce the fixed costs and may take place within a relatively short space of time.

It should be remembered that in the long-term there is no such thing as a fixed cost and that all costs are variable.

The segregation of costs into fixed and variable is not always an easy task. Some costs are semi-variable. If significant, the two elements have to be identified. Conflict may arise in a number of cases, for example:

	Variable cost	Fixed cost
Rent of equipment	Paid for by an amount based upon units produced	Paid for as a fixed amount
Direct labour: bonus	Based on production	Based on profits
Basic wage	(?)	(?)

It can be observed that the same item, e.g. rent of equipment or bonus, can be treated as either a fixed cost or a variable cost in certain circumstances. With the basic wage, it could be argued that because this will be paid whether production takes place or not, it is a fixed cost. On the other hand, because the direct labour is usually engaged in production it could be argued that the basic wage is a variable cost. In a lot of cases the truth of the matter is that time recording will still take place and it should therefore be possible to split the basic wage up between productive, i.e. a variable cost, and non-productive activities (i.e. idle time). Should idle time be classed as a fixed or a variable cost? This will depend upon the type of idle time, e.g. training new operatives may be classed as a fixed cost. However, the final decision on treatment will usually rest with the accountant. Subjective judgement is here again!

RELATIONSHIPS

There is no doubt about it, marginal costing calculations are relatively simple, in theory!

	Product N £000	% of Sales
Selling price	50	100
less variable cost	20	40
Contribution	30	60%*

* The 60%, i.e. the contribution as a percentage of sales, is better known as the profit volume ratio.

In competitive business situations sales are not always made at a uniform rate. Companies may have quite complex pricing strategies. The true position for just one of a company's products is likely to be a multitude of differing contributions arising from different customers/segments/markets. It is also unlikely that the variable cost per unit will remain static for the reasons already mentioned. Thus, the contribution per product will tend to be an average contribution.

THE TREATMENT OF FIXED COSTS

The marginal costing treatment of fixed costs is to a large extent an attempt to overcome the problems encountered in absorption costing re the apportionment of overheads. Marginal costing is really emphasizing the point that a lot of overheads vary more with time than output. Why go to all the trouble of using subjective judgement to apportion such overheads? How can subjective judgements produce objective results?

In marginal costing fixed costs are therefore treated as *period costs*, i.e. they are *not* absorbed into product costs. They are simply charged against the profits of the period in which they were incurred. They are excluded from stock valuations and do not therefore get carried forward into the next accounting period. Whereas with absorption costing fixed costs are absorbed and carried forward in stock valuations, i.e. treated as unexpired costs. This is the case, even though the period represented by quite a large proportion of the fixed costs has expired! Thus, with marginal costing the problem of under or over-absorption does not exist. Have you ever come across a marginal costing question which does attempt to split the fixed costs between products? It is unfortunate that certain questions which appear in textbooks and professional examinations do attempt to share the fixed costs between products! Why? Well, in my opinion this goes against marginal costing principles. It also propagates the idea that this is good accounting practice. But is it? I repeat the fact that many fixed costs vary more with time than output. To share them out *equitably* between products is to my mind unnecessary and impossible.

CHANGES IN VOLUME OR TYPE OF OUTPUT

It is quite easy to project straight lines onto graphs into the future or to a higher level of activity. In the complex environment in which firms operate there are no such easy answers. As pointed out earlier, pricing policies may be quite complex. Prices may be varied between customers, segments and target markets. Also, variable costs are quite likely to react in a number of different ways to changes in volume or type of output. Growth in sales can be dangerous. The additional contribution generated may be swallowed up by an increase in fixed costs! Management need to appreciate that the theory of cost behaviour, to a large extent, does not apply to the real world.

BREAK-EVEN ANALYSIS

The profit volume ratio can be used to compute a company's break-even point:

Fixed Costs ÷ Profit Volume Ratio = Break-Even Point

This is fine for a single product environment but becomes difficult to apply in a multi-product environment. Why? Because in marginal costing fixed costs should not be split up between products; marginal costing was designed to avoid this problem. To compute the break-even point in a multi-product environment an average profit volume ratio would have to be computed. This would be based upon a constant product-mix. The problem is that companies may not have a constant product-mix!

The limitations of break-even analysis is one of the areas which does tend to receive adequate coverage in cost and management accounting texts. Most of the assumptions on which it is based are really also limitations, e.g. a constant product mix; constant unit costs; constant selling prices etc. It must be remembered that:

- Managerial decisions may affect both fixed and variable costs.
- The product-mix cannot be forecast with accuracy.
- The levels of efficiency/productivity may not be constant.
- Companies do produce products for stock.
- It may not take the amount of capital tied up into account.
- The time horizon will affect the chart.
- Selling prices may have to fluctuate to attract sales.
- If output rises, sales may in fact decline.
- Fixed and variable costs may not behave as expected.

Break-even analysis is just one piece of information and should be used in conjunction with other data. It is a technique which is more suited to the short-term, particularly when one recalls its limitations. Beware of its simplicity!

Key factors

The first problem encountered in this area is one of terminology; the key factor is also called the governing factor, the limiting factor and the principal budget factor!

Question: What is a key factor?
Answer: When a factor is of such importance that it influences all the other budgets it is a key factor and must always be taken into account before the functional budgets are prepared.

Examples of key factors are:

1 Supply of, e.g. raw materials, finished goods.
2 Demand, e.g. sales demand.
3 Labour supply.
4 Production capacity.
5 Warehouse capacity.
6 Finance.
7 Government, e.g. restrictions, legislation.

The marginal costing technique used to evaluate the effect of key factors and to ensure that profits are maximized, is to express the contribution per unit of the key factor. However, not all key factors can be easily expressed in terms of units. A major consideration is that management may, by their actions, be able to do away with or reduce the constraint imposed by a particular key factor. Labour supply problems may be overcome by: over-time, shiftwork, incentives and employing sub-contractors. The action which management may take to combat governmental key factors is limited, e.g. consultations with members of parliament/government officials; involvement with pressure groups; the use of the media.

Conclusions

Marginal costing is a useful technique but there are certain dangers:

- It is dangerous to assume that if volume increases the fixed costs will remain unchanged. All costs are variable in the long term. If volume increases fixed costs may well increase. Fixed costs are not completely uncontrollable. Management can, by their actions, affect the amount of their fixed costs, e.g. sub-letting a portion of their factory.
- It is dangerous to assume that costs are easily divisible between fixed and variable costs. The practical reality is that the accountant may have to exercise subjective judgement in order to divide certain costs into their fixed and variable elements.
- It is dangerous to assume that variable costs will vary directly with output. All sorts of factors dictate otherwise, e.g. changes in technology, economic factors, social change etc.
- It is dangerous to assume that selling prices will be constant. Companies now have quite complex pricing policies and cannot ignore competition. Companies do, in fact, sell the same product at different prices to customers, segments and target markets.
- It is dangerous to assume a constant product mix. The product mix is affected by numerous factors, e.g. demand, seasons, advances in technology, etc.
- It is dangerous that a short-term measure, designed to generate an additional contribution, becomes a long-term policy. Once sales have been made at a particular price which covers marginal cost and makes some contribution towards the recovery of fixed costs, the customer may not be prepared to accept a price increase. Customers who find out about special low prices charged to other customers may press for price reductions!
- It is dangerous to price products using a marginal costing basis. Pricing ought to ensure that all products bear their fair share of the overheads and that all overheads are covered.
- It is dangerous to get carried away with the quest for sales growth. Marginal costing may be guilty of promoting sales growth at the expense of profitability. Companies who have gone overboard on market share/sales growth would be strongly advised to pay more attention to securing an adequate return on their capital employed.

However, marginal costing does have much to commend its use:

- Product costs and stock valuations are more realistic in that they consist of identifiable costs. Expired costs (fixed costs) are not treated as unexpired costs, i.e. fixed costs are not carried forward to subsequent accounting periods via stock valuations.
- If used with care and adapted to meet the diverse conditions which apply in a real life environment, marginal costing can be extremely useful. Marginal costing can be an aid to decision making, e.g. the recognition/evaluation of key factors and as a guide to assessing the effect of changes in volume or type of output.

Absorption v. marginal costing again

Brief reference was made to the absorption versus marginal costing saga in Chapter 6. In marginal (variable or direct) costing, variable manufacturing costs are allocated to products and included in the stock valuation.

Many writers have argued the cases for and against marginal costing for stock valuation for external reporting. However, in the UK the Statement of Standard Accounting Practice on Stocks and Work in Progress (SSAP 9), published by the Accounting Standards Committee, states that:

> In order to match costs and revenue, the cost of stocks and work in progress should comprise that expenditure which has been incurred in the normal course of business in bringing the product or service to its present location and condition. Such costs will include all related production overheads, even though these may accrue on a time basis.

The effect of SSAP 9 was to require absorption costing for external reporting purposes.

Although absorption costing is required for external reporting, the marginal costing versus absorption costing debate still continues. Marginal costing can be used for internal reporting.

According to Drury (1985) the arguments in support of marginal costing are as follows:

- Marginal costing provides more useful information for decision-making. This assumes that only in a marginal costing system are costs split between variable and fixed costs.
- Marginal costing removes from profit the effect of stock changes. That is, profits will follow sales, which is deemed more desirable.
- Marginal costing avoids fixed overheads being capitalized in unsaleable stocks.

His arguments in support of absorption costing are as follows:

- Absorption costing does not understate the importance of fixed costs. Where decisions are based on marginal costing it is possible to lose sight of the need to cover all fixed costs in the long run.
- Absorption costing avoids fictitious losses being reported, for example, where there are seasonal sales.

Horngren and Sorter (1962) developed the 'relevant cost theory of stock valuation', in which they emphasized that the choice of absorption or marginal costing depended on the particular circumstances, and that one method was not superior in all situations.

The following summary has been produced to provide a deeper insight.

ABSORPTION (TOTAL) COSTING

- Apportionment of overheads – uses subjective judgement as to which base is most appropriate, e.g. floor area versus cubic capacity.
- Absorption of overheads – problem re choice of overhead absorption rate, e.g. machine hour rate, labour hour rate, etc.
- Results in an under or over-absorption of overheads.
- Fixed costs are carried forward in stock valuations, i.e. treated as unexpired costs until the goods are sold.
- Old and new products are normally charged the same proportionate amounts for overheads, even though the more recently added lines cost far more to start up, (e.g. R & D).

Effect = to under value profits on old products, and understate the costs of bringing out the new product.

- Production cannot be achieved without incurring fixed costs, thus such costs are related to production and ought to be included in product costs (excludes selling and distribution and usually administration costs). This avoids the marginal costing illusion that fixed costs have nothing to do with production.
- Avoids fictitious losses. Goods produced and stocked for re-sale in the following period, e.g. fireworks, leisure equipment etc. (Using marginal costing all the fixed overheads attributable to the stock carried forward would have been written off as period costs in the earlier period.)
- Overcomes anomalies associated with marginal costing, e.g.

Machine on	Fixed monthly rental	*Or* Rental based on production
Marginal costing treatment	Fixed overhead	Variable overhead
Stock valuation	Excluded	Included

- Pricing-total selling price fixed to cover total cost plus profit. (Marginal costing could lead to lower prices.)
- Absorption costing – useful for 'matching' of costs and revenues per period, but may not be as useful in providing information for decision making purposes, as is marginal costing.

MARGINAL COSTING

- Treats fixed costs as period costs, and does not therefore carry them forward in stock valuations.
- No attempt is made to relate fixed costs, many of which are incurred on a time basis, with product costs.
- Does not require subjective judgements re absorption rates and methods of apportionment. *But* note, it is very difficult to separate fixed and variable costs in practice and also that in the long run all costs are variable.
- The problem of under or over-absorption of overheads disappears.
- Fictitious profits cannot arise due to fixed costs being treated as 'period costs' and written off in the period in which they were incurred, rather than being carried forward in unsellable stock.
- Avoids false sense of security, e.g. profit using absorption costing may be satisfactory, but this could be more than off-set by overheads under-absorbed.
- Marginal costing = simple.
- The use of the contribution as an aid to decision making, e.g. to attain the planned profit.
- Pricing can be done intelligently – based on the contribution required and taking key factors into account. However, problems may arise where managers are encouraged to under price their products, thus failing to make an adequate contribution to cover the fixed costs.
- Break-even analysis – a useful exercise, but note its limitations.

- Break-even is based on the mistaken belief that costs can be divided easily into fixed and variable elements. In the long run there is no such thing as a fixed overhead. All overheads are variable in the long run. Managers neglect the fact that fixed costs are not a necessary burden and they can be altered, e.g. in the case of land the area rentable can be changed.
- It tends to promote the idea that the only way to improve profitability is to increase sales volume rather than to increase the profit margin.

A summary of the features of marginal (direct) costing and absorption (full or total) costing is shown in Appendix D.

Stock valuation

With both absorption and marginal costing a decision has to be made about the way in which stocks are going to be valued, e.g. FIFO, LIFO, Average etc.

Mini Cases

1   AN ANTICIPATED PROFIT TURNS OUT TO BE A LOSS!

Comments made at the meeting called to consider an increase in the sales of product XT were:

'The sales increase will result in a greater contribution and therefore greater profits.'

'The increase which is being proposed should increase our market share by 10%.'

'We already cover all our fixed costs from our existing sales level. Any additional contribution received is simply pure profit.'

When someone asked about the effect on fixed costs of increasing the sales volume the reply he received was, 'Yes, I accept that in the long term our fixed costs will change but in the short term they will tend to remain unchanged'.

The meeting approved the increase in sales growth and the members present were all pleased with the outcome. All they had to do now was implement the decision and await the increase in profits.

Four months later

When the quarterly results were circulated, the members were in for a shock. Their anticipated profit had turned out to be a loss.

The management had been guilty of three sins:
(a) Going for sales growth without assessing the effects upon profitability. The assumption that an increase in sales will bring about an increase in profits does not always hold true.
(b) They failed to realize that there are step fixed costs.
(c) Relying on the figures produced by a costing section that had not fallen into this particular trap before!

2 RECOGNIZE YOUR KEY FACTORS

A costing section recognized that for the year ahead the supply of a particular material would be limited. This situation had been identified in good time and placed constraints upon the activities of the company.

With this knowledge the management accounting section were able to ensure that all the other budgets which were being prepared took this into account.

The action taken by the costing section to ensure co-operation and co-ordination appeared to be quite sound. However, they had in fact failed to remember that key factors are not static and that their effects can be reduced/overcome via management action, e.g. using substitute materials, reducing waste, improving design etc.

3 TO MAKE OR TO BUY

To assist the management in deciding between continuing to manufacture a component or purchasing it from an outside supplier the costing section provided the following information:

Manufacturing cost	Per unit
	£
Direct labour	54
Direct materials	117
Variable overheads	34
	£205
Price from outside supplier	£190

After careful consideration the management decided to discontinue production of the component and to buy it from the outside supplier.

Was this a good decision?

It must be remembered that the information which was provided by the costing section is just one of many factors which should be considered. In this particular case a number of problems did arise as a consequence of the decision. Immediately after the implementation of the decision there was a lot more idle machine capacity and more labour idle time. Keeping a tight control on quality also became a problem and returned consignments of components did on occasions result in stock outs and lost production. After six months the outside supplier increased the price of the components to £220 per unit!

Summary

The decision to use marginal costing in place of absorption costing or vice versa is a creative act. The two systems will most likely produce differing results and be responsible for a variety of conflicting decisions.

The bulk of this chapter was devoted to the reproduction of the critical review article. The conclusions section of the article does in fact act as a useful summary. Thus, this summary merely re-emphasizes some of the more important points made in the article and draws the reader's attention to the remainder of the material covered.

Although the SSAP 9 does not recommend the use of marginal costing for financial reporting purposes marginal costing can be used for cost and management accounting purposes/internal reporting.

Marginal costing treats fixed costs as period costs and in so doing avoids many of the problems encountered in absorption (full) costing. Fixed costs are not included in stock valuations and are not therefore carried forward into the future. However, it is not always easy to designate costs as variable costs or fixed costs. The distinction between variable costs and fixed costs is not always clear cut. In the real world of business, costs do not always behave as expected. The over simplification of marginal costing and break-even analysis can lead to false perceptions and poor decision making.

The summary provided about absorption costing versus marginal costing is proof that neither is better than the other. Both systems have much to commend their use and many problems associated with their use.

The first mini-case study was designed to show that sales growth can be a dangerous strategy, that fixed costs are not always a constant amount (even in the short-term) and that the figures produced by the costing section could lead to poor decision making.

The key factor and make or buy mini-cases were included to demonstrate that the cost information is just one factor which has to be taken into account in the decision making process. There are also numerous non-financial factors, e.g. management action to eliminate a key factor and the quality control of bought out components.

At least marginal costing does provide more realistic costs because the costs used can in many cases be identified with the product. However, companies have fallen into the trap described in mini-case 1 and their projected profit has ended up as a real live loss!

10

Product costing and costing methods

Product costing

A 'product cost' can mean different things. It could be considered 'a' figure; the derivation of which is to be found in a cost accountant's working papers. On the other hand, it may be a computer produced document, describing the product, its material contents by item and quantity, the operations required, the time and labour skills required, the scrap allowances, and the cost composition for each item, i.e. material; subcontract work; labour; manufacturing overheads – variable and fixed; administration and selling expenses – variable and fixed and the scrap allowance. The latter has, inevitably, more potential applications.

The development of product costs has many facets. They can be categorized into three main areas:

1 Stock accounting requirements.
2 Technical specification.
3 Cost specification.

STOCK ACCOUNTING REQUIREMENTS

Most manufacturing companies report profits, at least internally, more frequently than for statutory purposes. While the valuation of stocks for the annual accounts may be supported by a physical count, it is often the case that for, say monthly profit reporting, the stock valuation has been derived from 'stock movements', rather than the valuation of a physical count. This is especially true for 'work-in-progress'. Thus the method of stock accounting, where the stock valuation is derived, will influence the specification of the product cost. The end product may be easily defined, but may be less easily identified during its manufacture. To some extent, the cost accountant can form a definition based upon the definitions developed by the production control function's monitoring of production through the factory. The extent to which this is acceptable is dependent upon the frequency of monitoring, and the value added between each control point, and the accuracy of the information used by the production control system. One instance where the production data was not accurate enough was found in a hot forging company. It was found that (a) the quantities reported were those used in an incentive bonus scheme, (b) the quantities delivered were − 10%, and (c) weigh-counting was used, but the tare

91

weights of the bins and the accuracy of the scales were in doubt.

Swann (1986) provided an insight into how variances can arise between the book value of inventory, and the actual value calculated from a physical inventory. He suggested the basic causes were:

- The accounting system is separate from the inventory system.
- Unit costs are set illogically. Use of 'latest cost' or 'average cost' is more prone to error than the use of 'standard cost'.
- Incorrect accounting procedures.
- Conversions. Where units of measure require conversion, errors are likely to arise.
- Use of 'averages'.
- Inaccurate bills of materials.
- Computer program errors in the cost of sales calculation, logic errors in the cost system, etc. (See also Chapter 7 and the case of the half-million pound stock deficit.)

A different type of situation is faced when different elements of the final product are treated differently in stock accounting terms. For example, where standard components are assembled to each customer's specification, at least three alternative approaches may be taken:

1 Production may be monitored at both component manufacture stage and customer order stage. The total cost – however calculated – will be downdated on the sale of the final product.
2 Production may be monitored at component manufacture stage only. Only the components will be formally costed for stock accounting: the assembly costs will be written off as they occur. This may be quite satisfactory when there is a rapid throughput through the assembly area, but less so when it is in excess of one month.
3 Production is monitored by production control for the component, and the cost accountant 'monitors' assembly production by either a purpose-designed return, or via despatch notes/invoices.

All three alternatives imply different monitoring procedures by the different functions, and different requirements from the 'product cost'. The cost accountant must be creative in developing a stock accounting system which is consistent with the operational controls and the product cost.

TECHNICAL SPECIFICATION

The physical specification of the product is an area given little space in the literature. There is seldom a single way to manufacture an item, even within the same manufacturing plant. The technical specification is relevant to:

- The material type/quality and quantity.
- The scrap/wastage allowance of both the raw material and finished/part-finished items.
- The purchasing specification, that is, the supplier, quantity purchased, special purchase terms, purchase discount associated with number of materials, etc.
- The manufacturing route – the degree of specification will vary depending upon who prepared it, for example, a methods study department is likely to be more

specific than a production controller or estimator or works manager.
- The labour and/or equipment efficiency.
- The set-up time.
- The 'life' of consumable dies and/or tools and/or jigs and fixtures.
- Etc.

The accuracy and/or nature of the various components of the technical specification may vary. Some may be theoretically correct calculations at the time they were prepared, while others may be 'best current estimates', while others may be the results of actual current achievements. Where a variety of products are produced, the permutation of potential combinations expands dramatically.

The cost accountant can express his/her creativity in selecting the specifications to be used, although the choice may be restricted by what is available, or the benefits to be gained from a 'more accurate' cost. The more factors incorporated into the technical specification the more credible the final product cost will be to the technical personnel. Whatever permutation is selected, it is important that the specification, and in particular its limitations, are understood. A certain creativity must be demonstrated in interpreting the 'actual' results in the various areas, which may be reported in a manner different from that required for an exact comparison with a product cost. For example, labour performance figures may be by cost centre, rather than for individual products, which may pass through more than one department.

COST SPECIFICATIONS

The 'cost specification' will emerge from consideration of the stock accounting requirements, the techical specification, and the different costing principles explored in Chapter 2. Before continuing, however, it must be pointed out that certain financial accounting principles may be particularly relevant in some industries, and outweigh the more detailed costing principles. An interesting example is described by Lawrie (1986) on how an accounting standard was developed for capitalizing oil and gas exploration costs.

In creating the product cost, the cost accountant will initially establish their purpose and use. The 'costs' established may vary depending upon the use, and circumstances. They may vary as different principles are adopted or as 'facts' change. The cost accountant must be creative in order to meet the needs of the user. Different users have different needs. It is important that the figures provided are relevant to, and realistic to, the decision being made, and the circumstances prevailing.

One issue worthy of a mention is the allocation/apportionment of administration and selling costs to product costs. Dudick (HBR, 1987) said that over the past ten years, selling, general and administrative (SG & A) expenses have been rising as a percentage of the total cost of doing business. It is not unusual for SG & A to approach 50% or more of a company's manufacturing costs. In the high-technology sector, SG & A can easily approach 100% of manufacturing expenses!

Many manufacturing companies continue to make the mistake of relying on the 'one size fits all' methods of allocating/apportioning SG & A costs. Although the use of standardized, across-the-board methods simplifies SG & A cost accounting, they can distort the profitability of a company's different product lines and market segments.

Dudick suggests that each element of SG & A expenditure should be considered, and that a suitable apportionment base is found for each cost element, for apportioning to products or market segments. He made an important caveat: 'too much refinement may impose unjustifiable record-keeping costs', and suggests that in most cases the exercise need be carried out annually, when the financial plan is developed.

Product costing from a creative cost and management accounting point of view includes all of the creativity which abounds in the elements of cost (i.e. materials, labour, direct expenses and overheads).

Inadequate product cost analysis has been responsible for understating the profits on old product lines and overstating profits on new product lines. How could this happen? It could happen in an absorption costing system simply by selecting a particular method for apportioning indirect expenditure, e.g. research and development expenditure.

Inadequate product costing has been responsible for bad decisions, e.g. the decision to buy components from outside suppliers rather than manufacture them.

Costing methods

Dudick (1985) argues that there are two basic systems for identifying manufacturing costs with products: job costing and process costing.

JOB COSTING

Costs are accumulated by individual customer order because of the uniqueness of the product specifications required to fit the customer's needs. Dudick stated that,

> Although there is some advantage to making analytical studies through use of direct costing, companies making products that are unique to a customer should always give close attention to actual costs on a full costing basis.

A lot of job costing tends to be carried out on a historic basis (i.e. after the event). However, costing systems have to provide quotations which does involve predetermination. The competitive situation may, in fact, force a quote which is unjustified and uneconomical.

PROCESS COSTING

Costs are accumulated by process (usually identified by department or cost centre). No distinction is made by customer order because the products are standard and built to stock rather than to individual customer order.

He also identified three levels of costing:

1 *Primary costing level.* The basic costing system, i.e. job or process costing.
2 *Secondary costing level.* The option as to whether standard costs will be used rather than actual.
3 *Tertiary costing level.* The option as to whether direct costing or absorption (full) costing will be used.

Rotch and others (1982) developed a Matrix of Cost System Choices based on almost an identical taxonomy. (Dudick's 'Advantages and Disadvantages of Job and Process Cost Systems' is reproduced as Appendix E.)

The article which follows takes a critical look at process costing and indicates areas of creativity:

PROCESS COSTING – A CRITICAL VIEW

Can we really compute realistic and fair process costs? Process costing involves an attempt to compute the cost of a product for each process, operation or stage of manufacture. The products to which process costing applies may be produced by one or a number of processes.

Process costing involves:

1 *Process cost centres*
   The factory has to be divided up into process cost centres. The costs for each process cost centre in terms of materials, labour and overheads have to be collected and recorded in order to ascertain the cost of the process.
2 *The build up of product costs*
   Except in the case of a single process environment, the output of one process in effect becomes the raw material of the next process. Further material, labour and overhead costs will need to be added to the cost of production transferred from the previous process. In this way, the process costs are accumulated.
3 *Records*
   Records tend to be maintained in terms of *quantity* and cost. This is necessary in order to account for scrap, waste and losses. Thus, quantity reports should be prepared.
4 *Unit costs*
   The cost per unit of output is usually calculated and in its simplest form could be

$$\frac{\text{Process cost}}{\text{Number of completed units}} = Cost\ per\ unit$$

5 *Scrap and waste*
   Scrap tends to have some value and may or may not be used in further processing.
   Waste has no value and may be regarded as normal or abnormal. Normal losses tend to be absorbed by the completed units, whereas it is recommended that abnormal losses should be written off in the Costing Profit and Loss Account.
6 *Work-in-process* (work-in-progress)
   The technique devised to assist with the computation of the value of work-in-progress is called 'equivalent production'. This technique relies on the assessment of the differing degrees of completion for each element of cost, e.g.

Work-in-progress	Degree of completion
Materials	100%
Labour	60%
Overheads	60%

Knowing the degree of completion, units are converted into whole units, i.e. equivalent units (EU). This technique is perhaps better illustrated by the following example:

95

At the end of the month of January 19x8, 2000 units were still in progress. The degree of completion of these units was:

Input from previous process	100%
Conversion costs:	
Materials	60%
Labour	50%
Overheads	50%

The cost per unit is as follows:

Input from previous process	£3.80
Conversion costs:	
Materials	£10.00
Labour	£7.00
Overheads	£4.00

The solution is

	(a) WIP units	(b) Degree of completion	(a) × (b) Equivalent units	Cost £	Amount £
Input (previous process)	2 000	100%	2 000	3.80	7 600
Materials	2 000	60%	1 200	10.00	12 000
Labour	2 000	50%	1 000	7.00	7 000
Overheads	2 000	50%	1 000	4.00	4 000
			Value of work-in progress		£30 600

7 *Overhead absorption*
One of the key areas for later discussion is the old problem child, overheads. How should overheads be treated in a process costing environment?

8 *By-products and joint products*
By-products are produced incidental to the main/joint products. With joint products one or more products are processed but none of which can be regarded as the main product. Valuation has to be carried out at certain points of separation, e.g. the separation of a by-product from the main product at the end or during a particular process.

9 *Control by responsibility*
A manager or foreman will usually be in charge of a particular process cost centre. He/she will have to account for abnormal losses/efficiency variances etc.

10 *Applications*
When one hears the words process costing, one tends to think about its application to the chemical industry. However, it must be remembered that process costing could be and most certainly is used in numerous other industries, e.g. textiles, bread and biscuit making, various food products, paint manufacture, etc.

The critical review
Having listed the characteristics of process costing the time has now arrived to make a more critical appraisal.
   One question which must be asked at the outset is, 'What is the purpose of process costing?' This then raises a number of questions such as, is process costing trying to:
● Provide an accurate product cost?

- Provide accurate valuations of work-in-progress?
- Cover all the costs incurred in producing the product/s?
- Simply assign a value to production?
- Compute the contribution/s made by the product/s?
- Provide a basis for setting selling prices?

The process costing objective to my mind depends upon whether the company opts for absorption costing or marginal costing.

With absorption costing the process costing objective could well be, 'to ensure that *all* the costs of producing the products (direct and indirect) are covered and in so doing ensuring that realistic selling prices are set'.

With marginal costing the process costing objective could be, 'to ascertain the contribution made by each of the products produced'.

I believe that many users of process costing systems either never consider what the objectives of the system are, or have false perceptions of what the objectives are. Also, users may expect the process costing system to deliver something which it cannot deliver, e.g. precise costs in an absorption costing environment!

The direct labour and material input content to a process is a matter of fact and does not present any real costing problems. The real difficulty is once again a matter of dealing with overheads. Those overheads which can be identified with a process can be charged direct to it. With absorption costing those overheads which cannot be identified with a process will have to be charged to it using some abitrary base such as the number of direct labour hours. This introduces a high degree of subjectivity. This means that the costs computed cannot be regarded/described as accurate. To a large extent a marginal costing approach overcomes this problem.

The valuation of work-in-progress also involves consideration of which method of stock valuation to employ, e.g. FIFO, LIFO, average cost. Selection of the method tends to rest with the cost accountant. Someone must also estimate the degree of completion of the work-in-progress, the key word being estimate. Thus, there is quite an element of personal judgement in the evaluation of work-in-progress.

Another area worthy of note is the valuation of by-products and/or joint products at the point of separation, e.g. Fig. 10.1: the value of the by-product produced in Process I and the value of products X and Y produced in Process III.

Some of the methods used for by-products are:

1 Where the by-product is of little value the costs of producing the by-product just simply remain within the process in which it is produced. Any revenue received from selling the by-product is then credited to the process concerned or included in the profit and loss as miscellaneous income.
2 Where the by-product is treated as a separate product. The amount of by-product produced in a process will be transferred at an assigned value to a by-product account. It is the assigned value which poses the problem. Market value is just one value which could be used and one which is mentioned in numerous cost accounting texts. Not very sophisticated, is it?

The same problem arises in the assignment of a value at the point of separation for joint products. Some of the methods put forward for dealing with this problem are:

1   Quantitative. Using some form of physical measurement, e.g. weight. This however cannot be used in the case illustrated in Fig. 10.1 where one joint product is a liquid and the other is a solid. Where it is possible to weigh the products, to use weight alone could be quite misleading. Why? Because the joint products are different.
2   Market value. The use of the market value at the point of separation, if this information is available, does recognize the fact that joint products are different from each other. If the market value at the point of separation is not available the market value after further processing could be used.

Example
Zum and Gum are produced in Process 3. The total cost of Process 3 for the period was £8400. During the period 8000 tons of Zum and 4000 tons of Gum were produced. The market price of Zum was £1 per ton and the market price of Gum was £4 per ton.
   If the value at separation was computed on the basis of weight only the cost of Process 3 would be divided up between the two products as follows:

		£
Zum	8/12 × 8 400	5 600
Gum	4/12 × 8 400	2 800
		8 400

However, if market value was taken into account the cost of Process 3 would be divided between them:

		MARKET VALUE		£
Zum	8 000 × £1	8 000	8/24 × 8 400	2 800
Gum	4 000 × £4	16 000	16/24 × 8 400	5 600
		24 000		£8 400

Which do you think is the better method?
   Either way the selection of the method used to apportion the costs depends upon the judgement of the selector. The costs assigned to the joint products cannot be described as accurate costs because in many cases it is difficult to identify the material, labour and overhead content of each product.
   It is a fact that a by-product is different from the main product and that joint products are different from each other. Some of the methods proposed for assigning a value at the point of separation do take this into account, e.g. the use of a weighted market price. However, the methods described/proposed by numerous costing texts lack sophistication. Surely, in this age of rapid technological advance more sophisticated methods based upon technical data ought to be possible, e.g. with chemicals, by securing the co-operation of the scientists.
   One area which does not pose too much of a problem in process costing is the identification of production cost centres. Production cost centres can be clearly defined as they tend to be processes.
   The valuation of work-in-progress using the equivalent production method does provoke some thought. It may, in many cases be extremely difficult to estimate the degree of completion with accuracy. In many processes, additional raw materials are added throughout the process. How complete is the work-in-progress as regards the overheads? One method of absorbing

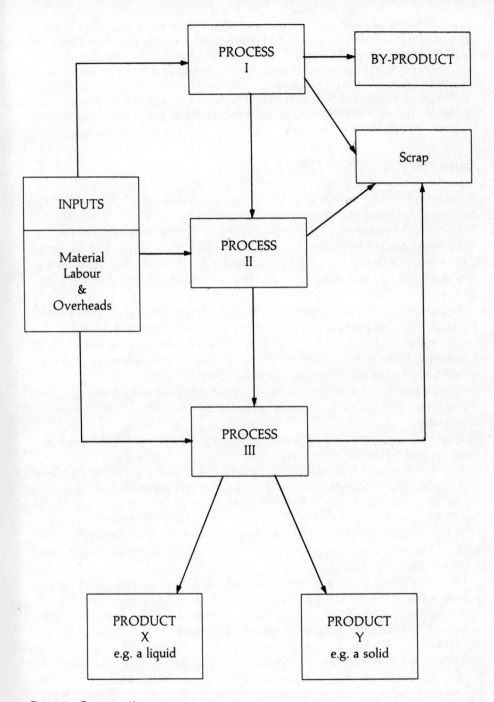

Fig 10.1   Process costing

overheads into process costs is to use a direct labour hour basis. The point that can be made here is, yes a lot of overheads vary with time and a time based method would appear to be appropriate. However, it must be remembered that the overheads are pre-determined and that a lot of those overheads vary more with the level of activity than they do with time. Process costs can be computed with reasonable accuracy up to the marginal cost. However, to use absorption costing is a different ball game and does involve subjective choices by individuals.

Summary

In this chapter three aspects of product costing were discussed. They were stock accounting, technical specification and cost specification.

It should be noted that for monthly/quarterly internal reporting purposes the stock figures tend to be derived figures. On occasions the inadequacy of production data means that the figures produced are inaccurate. However, the figures that are produced, accurate and inaccurate, do have an influence on product cost specifications.

Swann (1986) provides an insight into the possible reasons for differences between the book stock and physical stock, e.g. conversions, computer program errors, etc.

The monitoring procedures employed within an organization may demand/influence different requirements of the product cost. Certain elements of the final product may be treated differently in stock accounting terms.

With the technical specification the degree of accuracy will depend to a large extent upon the quality of the information available/ability of whosoever has prepared it.

With the cost specification the cost accounting section need to be creative in order to serve the needs of the user.

Here also, the point was made about the difficulty in dealing with fixed overheads and in particular the treatment of selling, general and administration costs. The treatment of such costs can distort the profitability of product lines and market segments.

Product costing provides vast scope for creativity because it comes face to face with all the creative aspects of the elements of cost, i.e. materials, labour, direct expenses and overheads.

Dudick (1985) argues that there are really just two systems of identifying manufacturing costs; job costing and process costing.

Even though a lot of job costing takes place on a historic basis the costing personnel still have to provide quotations. Quotations which have to be pre-determined and also take account of the competitive situation.

There is a lot of scope for the creative cost and management accountant and his/her staff in the process costing area. Numerous subjective judgements have to be made about scrap, waste, overheads, by-products, joint products, work-in-progress, etc.

To complete this summary the conclusions section of the critical review article is now reproduced.

Conclusions
The result of the review is a lot of questions, such as:

- What is the objective of process costing?
- What is the objective of assigning costs to by-products and joint products?
- How should normal and abnormal losses be treated?
- Can the degree of completion of work-in-progress be estimated with accuracy in terms of materials, labour and overheads?
- Should the company employ a marginal costing or an absorption costing approach?
- With absorption costing, how are the overheads to be absorbed into process costs?
- Which method/s should be used to assign processing costs to joint-products at the point of separation?
- Just how accurate are the process costs?

Companies have been known to discontinue the manufacture of products simply because of the way in which accountants have computed the figures! Thus, care must be exercised particularly where there is an absorption/process costing type system which involves by-products/joint products.

There is a real need for more sophisticated methods to be developed if process costs are to be used for decision making purposes.

Further views on Joint and By-Product Costing are contained in Appendix F.

11

Pre-determined costing – budgets and standards

Budgeting

Budgetary control
'The establishment of budgets relating the responsibilities of executives to the requirements of a policy, and the continuous comparison of actual with budgeted results either to secure by individual action the objective of that policy or to provide a basis for its revision.'

A budget
'A financial and/or quantitative statement, prepared and approved prior to a defined period of time, of the policy to be pursued during that period for the purpose of attaining a given objective. It may include income, expenditure and the employment of capital.'

The aims of budgetary control are the:
- Planning of business policy.
- Co-ordination of all business activities.
- Control of each function to achieve optimum efficiency.
- Recognition of individual responsibility.

Creativity may arise at the outset as a direct result of the inability of management to communicate their objectives clearly. The cost and management accountant and the functional heads of department will all have their own perceived ideas as to what the objectives are.

It was pointed out in Chapter 2 that the activity of predetermination provides great scope for creativity. Numerous variables have to be considered and assumptions made about future changes in the environment. Again, a considerable amount of subjective judgement has to take place. Subjectivity means greater creativity.

In many cases the starting point of the budgeting process is the sales budget. The management accountant has to rely heavily on the information provided by the marketing/sales staff. The sales forecast must therefore be prepared with great care. This is because all budgets are inter-related. The volume of sales helps to determine the volume of production. The volume of production helps to determine the material requirements budget, and so on.

The setting of targets for sales, production etc. does affect the behaviour of the personnel involved. The levels of activity which have to be set have a significant impact upon overhead recovery rates in an absorption costing environment. To predetermine future levels of activity with accuracy is not an easy task.

In the capital budgeting decision the planning of future capital expenditure must include an assessment about changes in technology. In many cases the machinery/equipment that will be needed in a few years time is not yet on the market!

Sales is not always the starting point in the budgeting process because it may not be the principal budget factor (also called the key factor, limiting factor or governing factor). This area was covered in Chapter 9 in relation to marginal costing. The principal budget factor has to be taken into account first when preparing budgets because it constrains what can be done.

Remember that management action can obliterate/reduce the effects of the principal budget factor, e.g. if it happens to be the supply of labour it may be overcome by: overtime, shiftwork, using robots, new incentive schemes, etc.

The role of the cost and management accountant as a gatekeeper was described in Chapter 1. The cost and management accounting functions provide a lot of information to assist the other functions in the preparation of their budgets. They can therefore, control the flow of information and therefore exercise considerable influence over the budgets produced. They also tend to have the control over the flow of budget communications and budget reports both upwards, downwards and sideways. Decisions have to be made relating to what is to be classed as an exception (so that it can be brought to the attention of management) in the management by exception reporting system. It must also be noted that if the communications from the costing selection are unclear this could create havoc. Bad communications can be very creative!

An area which demands creativity on the part of the cost and management section is the resolution of conflicting departmental objectives. It is quite a natural phenomenon for departments to be fighting amongst themselves for resources. They all want a larger slice of the cake. The costing section have to perform a balancing act in order to satisfy the competing forces. The costing section will be called upon to produce figures to assist management in making their resource allocation decisions. It must be remembered that each department has its own objectives and that individuals within departments have their own personal objectives. These departmental and personal objectives may conflict with the objectives set by management!

Budgeting depends upon control by responsibility. Decisions have to be made regarding who is going to be responsible for a particular budget. These decisions could affect performance and industrial relations, e.g. the perceived authority of the responsible person, the pressure to which the responsible person is subjected.

It is common knowledge that flexible budgets, i.e. those which are designed to change to reflect differing levels of activity are preferable to fixed budgets, i.e. those which do not change in line with the level of activity.

If the fixed budget was adopted it would be auto-creative, i.e. variances would arise by comparing different levels of activity (unless the fixed budget and actual just happened to be the same).

Standard costing

Setting a standard cost for a product follows a similar procedure to costing a job using planned figures in place of actuals.

Standard costing might be defined as the conversion of efficiency records into cost records. The establishment of standards involves:

- Specifications of material to be used.
- Allowable quantity of material (including scrap allowance).
- Standard material prices.
- Types of operations and equipment required.
- Time allowances for operation – these can be based upon:
  - estimates based on past performance adjusted for the unusual
  - time studies
  - predetermined tables of allowances.
- Standard labour rates by nature of operation.
- Predetermined overhead rate(s).

The advantages and disadvantages of standard costing can be summarized as follows:

Advantages
- Simplified record keeping.
- Permits the use of variances as a management control.
- Control information available more frequently.

Disadvantages
- Requires constant maintenance – keeping standards up to date, particularly in a period of high inflation.
- May produce standards which are small in volume and run only once.

Which standard should be used?

There are a number of standards from which to choose, e.g. ideal standards, expected standards. A selection has to be made. Assessing what is ideal or expected or attainable is highly subjective.

As with budgeting what is reported and how it is reported upwards/downwards is determined by the cost and management department.

Conclusions

The creative aspects of materials, labour, direct expenses, overhead and costing methods all apply to budgets and standards. Additional creativity results from the predetermination process.

Further creativity may result from failing to monitor/review the systems at frequent intervals and the failure to amend the budgets/standards because of changes in basic assumptions.

Mini cases

1   ACROSS THE BOARD CUTS

The organization had been going through a bad patch. Management had agreed to a 10% reduction in the capital expenditure budget for the forthcoming year. It was clear from the meetings held that all of the departments concerned were most unwilling to take a cut in their budget. The cost and management accountant looking for an easy way out drew up a proposed budget which incorporated a ten per cent cut across the board. This was accepted and implemented.

This compromise was not a very good decision. It created a situation where the weak became weaker and the strong also became weaker!

2   UNATTAINABLE SALES TARGETS

Each member of the direct sales force had a budgeted sales target to meet each month for their particular area. Although the sales made by the sales person for the north-eastern section were up by 5% on last year, they were still ten per cent below budget. The sales person concerned lost out on commission during the year and was dismissed from the job because of his/her inability to reach the targets set.

Were the targets for this area set too high? Had the basic assumptions about the economic climate in that area changed? Were the targets set for other areas too low?

The budget system could bring about injustice.

Summary

In the budgeting/standard costing area creativity may stem from:
- The perceptions of the objectives set by management.
- The process of the predetermination of costs, revenues and output, etc.
- The assumptions made about the future economic environment and changes in technology.
- Target setting (see mini-case 2 – an example of how it could cause an injustice).
- The computation of the level of activity.
- The principal budget factor being regarded as immovable.
- The role of 'gate keeper', i.e. control over the flow of information/communications upwards, downwards and sideways.
- The difficulty in defining exception in management by exception.
- The resolution of conflict. This could lead to sub-optimal decisions being made, e.g. as illustrated in mini-case 1.
- The allocation of responsibility.
- The use of fixed budgets.
- Failure to monitor, review and revise budgets and standards.
- The assessment of standard prices and standard quantities.
- The selection of the appropriate standard, e.g. ideal or expected standard.

The creativity which has already been mentioned in relation to the elements of cost and other costing methods also applies because they also may be subject to pre-determination.

Part 4

Decision making

12

Creative decision making

Rayburn (1986) emphasized that different costs should be used for different purposes and that merely collecting cost accounting data does not completely fulfil the accountant's responsibility. When management is faced with choosing between alternative courses of action, and the costs collected using conventional accounting procedures are inadequate, the accountant may be asked to prepare a special cost study. Many of the costs which are likely to be used, such as differential costs, opportunity costs or replacement costs, are never entered in formal accounting records.

Decision making is the process of studying and evaluating two or more available alternatives, leading to a final choice. It is intimately involved with planning for the future and is directed towards a specific objective or goal. Costs must be tailored to fit the specific problem and only relevant costs should be considered. However, determining which costs are relevant is often debatable and the result is, at best, an estimate. Relevant costs are generally those which will respond to managerial decision-making, but they vary with individual projects and the length of the project planning period.

Horngren (1977) emphasized relevant costs and the contribution approach to decisions. He said that:

> Historical costs in themselves are irrelevant to the decision, although they may be the best available basis for predicting future costs.

Drury (1985) also introduced the concept of relevant costs:

> Relevant costs are future costs that differ amongst alternatives.

He also thought it was necessary to take qualitative factors into account.

Horngren also distinguished between qualitative and quantitative factors. Qualitative factors are those whose measurement in value terms is difficult and imprecise; yet a qualitative factor may easily be given more weight than the measurable cost savings. For example, a militant trade union that opposes the introduction of some labour saving machinery may cause an executive to defer or to reject completely the contemplated installation.

Some illustrations of relevance are described below:

Activity levels: Decisions that affect activity levels are made under a given set of conditions, including existing plant capacity, equipment and basic operating conditions. Such decisions are essentially short-run in nature; but they have long run overtones that should never be overlooked.

Fixed expenses/unit costs: In most cases it is safer to compare total costs and revenues rather than the unit amounts.

Short/long run: Horngren advised that one should

> not jump to the conclusion that all variable costs are relevant and all fixed costs are irrelevant. Economists and accountants agree that if the length of time under consideration is long enough, no type of cost is fixed.

Keys (1986) found that overhead apportionments were not accurate and caused poor decisions. He found that much of the inaccuracy was caused by the use of direct labour hours and direct labour cost as an overhead base (two symptoms of the problem were extremely high and volatile overhead rates) and the activity level used to calculate the overhead rate was hard to forecast and was not usually adjusted more frequently than every year. He also considered that the best interpretation of overhead absorbed by a job or product is that it is a crude approximation for the costs the company has to cover in the long run to remain operating.

He also found that some companies used plant-wide or even company-wide overhead rates which led to inaccurate overhead allocations. Companies had departments which were fundamentally different with respect to how overhead costs were incurred. The departments had different activity levels and should have had different overhead bases.

The reasons for inaccurate overhead absorption rates were: the overhead base, relevance of recorded costs, activity level, and departmental versus company-wide rates.

Keys (1986) also suggested that the solution to problems caused by using direct labour hours and cost as an overhead base was to use machine hours as the overhead base.

With problems such as make-or-buy decisions, Rayburn (1986) said that historical costs had such serious limitations that they could not be used for short term planning. Instead, 'differential costs' (that is, those costs that change with alternatives) should be used as a basis for decision making, the objective of which is to make better use of existing facilities to increase profits or reduce losses. However, she pointed out that:

> a cost study prepared for a make-or-buy decision should merely indicate the direction of a decision. Other factors such as trade secrets, seasonal sales, production fluctuations and the quality and design of the product must be considered, and *the application of make-or-buy principles should not overshadow more complicated problems facing management.*

Most managers are continually weighing alternatives. Decisions must be made not only when problems exist but also when opportunities have arisen. Opportunities can be considered as problems which must be solved in regard to the company's objectives, environmental conditions and outcomes. In decision making managers should attempt to incorporate a subjective evaluation of opportunity cost into the final decision.

Replacement cost may also be useful in cost studies. However its use in a routine costing system can, according to Rayburn, be difficult to apply. Like opportunity costs, replacement costs can be highly subjective. For example, the replacement cost of productive facilities will require assumptions whether the existing facilities are replaced as they are, or whether new technology is employed.

The traditional types of cost-data collected may no longer be appropriate. Pyne (1986) believes that the environment faced by high technology industries requires that their management accountants acquire new skills re:

1 Life-cycle costing – to meet the phenomenon of shorter product, plant and facilities life cycles.
2 Costs outside the producer's business – for transport, warehousing, distribution, marketing and sales efforts.
3 Estimating competitors' cost structures – in meeting the increasing global competitive challenges.
4 Programme and project accounting – for monitoring new product launches, repositioning strategies etc.
5 Programme analysis and cost/benefit review methods – in order to evaluate the introduction of CAD and/or CAM integrated manufacturing systems, etc. (CAD – Computer Aided Design, and CAM – Computer Aided Manufacture.)

He also suggested:

1 A revised basis for unit operating cost ascertainment: namely that the costs of facilities and station staffing, energy provision and supplies may be matched with products on the basis of 'product residence' at each work, move, or hold station.
2 A revised classification of costs: namely that costs are classified into categories which indicate the kind of decision which needs to be taken to change levels of cost.

He suggested grouping costs under the following headings:
- Committed costs.
- Costs of idle, under-used or abandoned capacity or facilities.
- Programme or policy costs.
- Managed costs.
- Market rate related costs.
- Environmental costs.
- Direct costs.
- Common costs.

Quite a number of the mini-cases/other cases described in this book are practical illustrations of creative decision making.

Summary

This chapter took on the form of a review of selected literature relating to decision making.

Decision making usually needs more information than that which is collected for conventional accounting purposes. Indeed, many costs such as opportunity costs, replacement costs and differential costs never really enter into the formal accounting records.

Decision making involves choosing between a number of alternatives. Strong recommendations from leading authors/cost and management accountants advocate the use of 'relevant costs', i.e. those costs which are affected by managerial decision-making. Qualitative factors cannot and should not be ignored. This view was supported by Drury (1985) and Horngren (1977). The assessment of qualitative factors is an area in which there is great scope for creativity.

Yet again the difficulty involved in using absorption costing and the difficulty of assessing the level of activity was also highlighted.

Pyne (1986) came up with a list of skills which he considered cost and management accountants should acquire in order to keep pace with environmental change in high-tech industries.

If we agree that such skills are necessary, we also accept that there is a deficiency in the training of cost and management accountants. The knowledge gap identified could well result in creativity!

13
Creative capital investment appraisal

This chapter consists of three articles covering the selection of discount rates, taxation and non-financial factors.

Creativity arises as a consequence of having to make selections, the pre-determination of cash flows, the assumptions, the treatment of risk and qualitative judgements re the non-financial factors.

CAPITAL INVESTMENT APPRAISAL – WHICH DISCOUNT RATE? 'I propose that we evaluate this particular project using the discounted cash flow approach', said the Production Director. 'And which discount rate would you propose that we use?' commented the Finance Director. 'Oh, I think that we can quite easily leave all of that in the capable hands of your accounts department', interrupted the Managing Director.

How true a reflection is this, of your own situation and experience?

It is an indisputable fact that in the real world of industry and commerce accountants are frequently confronted with the problem of selecting an appropriate discount rate. It is, however, unlikely that a lot of time and thought is devoted to this highly subjective area. The selection of a discount rate is a time consuming and complex process.

Why discount?
Money has a 'time value', i.e. a £1 today will be worth more than a £1 in the future: using a 10% discount rate £1 today will be worth 90.9p in one year's time.

This is caused by a number of factors such as consumer preferences, investment opportunities, risk and impact of inflation.[1]

The discounting technique provides the accountant with a method by which cash flows can be adjusted to take into account the time value of money.

Discounting the cash flow, it must be said, is just one of a number of factors which must be assessed during the capital investment decision making process, e.g. there are numerous non-financial factors.[2]

The selection of a discount rate
There are a multitude of rates from which a selection can be made.

The cost of capital
'Oh, as a rule of thumb, I would just use the cost of capital as our discount

rate', propounded the Company Secretary.

This simplistic approach is just not on. Quite a number of authorities advocate the adoption of the cost of capital as an appropriate discount rate. The principal concern here arises from the fact that there are in existence several ways of computing a company's cost of capital. One further complication is that a decision will have to be reached about whether to use the before or after tax cost of capital!

The weighted average cost of capital is a method which reflects the current gearing and tends to be used in cases where the same structural financial mix is going to continue.

If the gearing is likely to change in the future, then it would seem that the anticipated future weighted average cost of capital would be preferable.

It is difficult to determine changes to the future structural mix, e.g. caused by environmental change such as competition, economic, political and technological factors. The weighting may be based on book values or market values (see Fig. 13.1). However, it is generally agreed that a cost based on market values may give a more accurate picture in times of changing values.

Figure 13.1 illustrates that differences between the two methods can occur. Such differences could be quite significant! The computation of the cost figures via the formulae is open to differing interpretations and highly debatable. Growth rates have to be pre-determined, taxation must be taken into account and market price/market value selections made. In addition to affecting a company's gearing, any new financing may also have an impact upon the company's risk profile.

An alternative to the weighted average cost method is to use the marginal cost method.

The marginal cost of capital is the total change in the cost of the finance incurred through a new project. This method is considered to be appropriate in cases where a project is financed from a specific source and the source utilized does not correspond to the financing proportions that the firm intends to use in the future.

It is however, extremely difficult to identify the cost of financing a particular project, because several projects may be commissioned at the same time using finance from a variety of sources.

The cost of capital, weighted or marginal, as a discount rate is useful in that if the project under review achieves a positive net present value (NPV) it is worthy of further consideration. The cost of capital is, as indicated, a highly subjective area.

Cut-off rates
A frequently adopted alternative to the cost of capital as the discount rate is the cut-off rate. Management have to agree upon the cut-off rate/s to be employed. This method is useful in times of capital rationing and where numerous projects have to be screened. Projects with a negative NPV are automatically rejected and those with positive NPV's proceed for further consideration. A drawback to this method is that projects which fall below the cut-off but above their cost of capital are simply ignored.

Risk-adjusted discount rates
There are a number of ways in which the risk factor may be dealt with. The cut-off method can be extended to take the project's risk category into account. It is therefore, possible that company's employ differential cut-offs, e.g.

	Project risk	Discount rate
	:-----------	:------------
	Low	12%
	Average	17%
	High	25%

Thus, the higher the risk, the higher the discount rate. Risk assessment is a difficult matter and here also, subjectivity is brought into play. This method is suitable for real world situations. Management do in fact have to make their selections from numerous projects with differing classifications.

Internal rate of return

'Why not dispense with the discount rate/NPV approach and simply evaluate alternatives according to their respective internal rates of return?' said the Management Accountant.

A very good question. This would free the personnel concerned from having to decide upon which discount rate to adopt. Projects can be ranked according to their internal rate of return (IRR) and risk category. A quite recent survey indicated that this technique has found wide acceptance in the real world.[3] Of the firms surveyed 41% were using IRR as their primary method of appraisal.

Cash flows

It should be noted that cash flows which are being discounted are only estimates. Their calculation should, one hopes, have taken inflation and taxation into account. Cash flows, it must also be pointed out do not accrue evenly throughout the year and it may be necessary to adjust discount rates accordingly.

It would appear that a perception of accuracy occurs when the cash flows are multiplied by the discount factor. Beware, the cash flows are still estimates and the discount factor the outcome of subjective judgement.

Guidelines and conclusions

The selection of an appropriate discount rate should therefore, take into account the following considerations:

1   The weighted average method is suitable for situations where the current financing structural mix is going to continue. Where that mix is likely to change an attempt should be made at calculating the anticipated cost of the new structure.
2   Weighted averages based on market values tend to give a better reflection of the cost of capital during periods of changing values, i.e. the usual real world situation.
3   If at all possible, identify the source/cost of the funds which will be used to finance a particular project.
4   Do not ignore the risk factor. Take risk into account, e.g. by adjusting discount rates accordingly.
5   We live in a world with taxation, so take the impact of tax into account when computing the discount rate.
6   The discounting process is just one component part of the capital investment decision making process. It is most certainly not the be all and end all.
7   It does not matter which discount rate is used, if the cash flows are way out of line and based upon improper assumptions.
8   The adoption of the internal rate of return technique avoids many of the problems associated with the selection of discount rates. It is a method which merits attention.

9   A post-audit/monitoring process should be instigated to provide
    management with valuable feedback upon projects in progress.
On the face of it, it would appear that the selection of an appropriate discount
rate is an easy matter. This is not so, subjective judgements are never easy
and several variables have to be considered. The only certainty is, that it will
continue to puzzle and perplex the accountancy profession for many years to
come.
    Which discount rate do you use?

Weighted average cost of capital

(a)	(b)	(c)	(d)	(e)
Method	Book value £m	Proportion %	Cost £	Weighted cost, £ (c × d)
Debentures	30	30	(a) 5	1.5
Preference	20	20	(b) 8	1.6
Ordinary	30	30	(c)12	3.6
Retained	20	20	(d)10	2.0
Earnings	100	100		8.7

If market values were used the position would be:

(a)	(b)	(c)	(d)	(e)
Method	Market value £m	Proportion %	Cost £	Weighted cost, £ (c × d)
Debentures	30	20	(a) 5	1.00
Preference	20	13.33	(b) 8	1.07
Equity	100	66.67	(c)12	8.00
	150	100		10.07

The above cost figures have been arrived at by employing the following
formulae:

(a) Debentures $= \dfrac{\text{Coupon rate}}{\text{current market price}} \times (1 - \text{tax rate})$

(b) Preference shares $= \dfrac{\text{coupon rate}}{\text{market price}} \times 100$

(c) New equity (ordinary) $= \dfrac{\text{dividend per share}}{(\text{market price} - \text{issue costs})} + \text{growth rate}$

(d) Retained earnings $= \dfrac{\text{dividend per share}}{\text{market price}} + \text{growth rate}$

Fig 13.1   *Weighted costs of capital calculated using book values and market values*

1 Pike R. H. & Dobbins R. *Investment Decisions and Financial Strategy.* Philip Allan Publishers, 1986.
2 Chadwick, L. 'Money doesn't mean everything'. *Accountants Weekly.* 12 June 1981.
3 Pike, R. H. *Capital Budgeting in the 1980s. ICMA,* 1982.

Further reading
Knott, G. *Understanding Financial Management.* Pan, 1985.

Capital investment appraisal and the tax factor

The tax factor always has, and always will, play an important role in the capital investment decision making process. In view of the fact that first year capital allowances on plant and machinery have now been phased out (Fig. 13.2),

	Rate
Up to 13 March 1984	100%
14 March 1984 to 31 March 1985	75%
1 April 1985 to 31 March 1986	50%
On and after 1 April 1986	Nil

Fig 13.2   Rates of first year capital allowances on plant and machinery

one would think that taxation would have little impact. This is not the case. Many commentators, managers and students tend to talk as though all of the capital allowances relating to plant and machinery have been axed. However, it must be remembered that the 25% writing down allowance is still available. It is allowable from the first year in which the expenditure takes place on cost and from the second year onwards on the written down value brought forward. This reducing balance method of capital allowances is no stranger, it has been in use for years and years in the area of cars capable of private use. In the year of sale, no writing down allowances are computed and claimed. The sale proceeds received are compared with the plant and machinery's written down value brought forward. The difference between the two figures being a balancing charge (on a profit on sale) or a balancing allowance (resulting from a loss on sale), tax being payable on any balancing charge or repayable on any balancing allowance.

I have observed quite a number of off-beat attempts at computing the taxation impact upon the discounted cash flow method of capital investment appraisal. To my mind, taxation should be taken into account during the process of estimating the incremental cash flows. After all, cash flow is all about time lags, i.e. the points in time when cash comes in or goes out. Taxation, from a cash point of view is no different. There is a time lag between the tax being paid/repaid and the income being generated.

I would like to propose that the following systematic method be considered, not just from an exam technique point of view but also from a practical point of view:

1   Estimate the incremental taxable cash flows (excluding taxation effects).
2   Work out the capital allowances over the life of the project taking into account the estimated residual value of the plant and machinery at the end of the project.
3   Deduct the capital allowances from the incremental cash flow, and then work out the tax payable or repayable by multiplying the net taxable incremental cash flow by the appropriate rate of Corporation Tax. You have now calculated the tax payable/repayable.
4   Taking into account the time lag for the payment/repayment of tax deduct the tax payable or add the tax repayable to the appropriate incremental cash flows, (taxable and non taxable).
5   Select an appropriate discount rate taking into account the tax factor. This is not an easy task and requires a great deal of time and thought.

Mini case study

The following mini case study using real world tax rates should help with the quest towards gaining an understanding of the impact of taxation upon the capital investment decision.

Your company, Ingwik PLC, is considering disposing of an old machine and replacing it by purchasing a new and more efficient machine.

You are provided with the following information:

The old machine

Life	6 years
Purchased	4 years ago
Cost	£36000
Residual value 1 July 1987	£3000
Tax written down value	Nil
Book value (after depreciating at 1/6 per annum straight line)	£12000
Residual value at the end of its life, i.e. end of year 31 December 1988	Nil

The new machine

Life	(approx) 5 years
Cost	£84000
Residual value at the end of 31.9.1991	£14000

Depreciation at 1/5 per annum straight line will be charged.

Date of purchase The company is proposing to buy the machine on 1 July 1987.

Taxation assumptions
1   If the machine is purchased outright capital allowances will be available at the appropriate rates.
2   Tax payments (and refunds, if any) are made in the year following that to which they relate.

3   The company's rates of corporation tax are those which are applicable to large companies.

Cost of capital The company's net of tax cost of capital is 10%.

Incremental cost savings are estimated to be as follows:

Year	New machine purchased
31.12.1987	£12000
31.12.1988	£23000
31.12.1989	£39000
31.12.1990	£37000
31.12.1991	£21000

You are required to prepare discounted cash flow statements and advise your company as to which course of action should be taken.

SUGGESTED SOLUTION

Step 1   The estimated incremental cash flows excluding the effect of taxation have already been computed.

Step 2   *The computation of the capital allowances*

Year ending	Cost of written down value b/f	Writing down allowance	Written down value (WDV) c/f
31.12.87	84000	21000	63000
31.12.88	63000	15750	47250
31.12.89	47250	11813	35437
31.12.90	35437	8859	26578

Year ending 31.12.87 Disposal of old machine

Sale proceeds	£3000
less	
Tax written down value	Nil
Balancing charge	£3000

Year ending 31.12.91 Disposal of new machine

Sale proceeds	£14000
less	
Tax written down value	26578
Balancing allowance	£12578

*Note that depreciation, being a non-cash item, does not have any effect whatsoever upon the outcome.

Step 3   *Calculation of the tax payable/repayable*

Year ending	(a) Cash flow	(b) Capital allowances	(c) Net taxable cash flow (a − b)	(d) Rate of corporation tax	(e) Tax (payable)/ repayable (c × d)
	£	£	£		£
31.12.87	12000	18000*	(6000)	35%	2100 Refund
31.12.88	23000	15750	7250	35%	(2537)
31.12.89	39000	11813	27187	35%	(9515)
31.12.90	37000	8859	28141	35%	(9849)
31.12.91	21000	12578 (BA)	8422	35%	(2948)

* (21000 less 3000 balancing charge)

119

Step 4   The discounted cash flow computation

Year ending	Cash flow	Tax (payable)/repayable	Net	Net of tax discount rate	DCF
		(Approx 1 Year)			
31.12.87	12000	(Time Lag)	12000	0.909	10908
31.12.88	23000	2100	25100	0.826	20733
31.12.89	39000	(2537)	36463	0.751	27384
31.12.90	37000	(9515)	27485	0.683	18772
31.12.91	35000*	(9849)	25151	0.621	15619
31.12.92	–	(2948)	(2948)	0.564	(1663)
					91753

less Initial cost (£84000 less amount received for old machine £3000)   81000

Net present value   10753

* £21000 + residual value of new machine £14000

NOTE

1   The discount rates for 31.12.87 and 31.12.91 could be amended to take into account the fact that the periods covered by the cash flows are six months and nine months respectively.
2   It is a very difficult task to estimate the incremental cash flows.
3   It is possibly even more difficult to estimate the future residual value of plant and machinery. Because of unforeseen advances in technology the machine considered in this mini-case could be significantly less than the figure currently estimated.
4   The actual date on which the tax would be paid over could vary considerably because of audit delays/appeals etc.
5   There are many other factors other than the financial factors which must be taken into account during the capital investment decision making process.

CONCLUSION

In the capital investment decision the tax factor must not and should not be ignored.

Money doesn't mean everything

THE NON-FINANCIAL ASPECTS OF CAPITAL INVESTMENT APPRAISAL

'The return on the project is greater than the firm's cost of capital, I therefore recommend acceptance of the project.' Is the capital investment decision really so easy and clear cut? There is a real danger for accountants to be so preoccupied with the financial aspects of capital investment appraisal that they may ignore other very important factors. Although these factors omitted may be described as non-financial and subject to qualitative decisions they could have quite a marked effect upon the firm's long term financial performance.

The various methods used by accountants to evaluate projects do have a number of limitations. Cash flows have to be estimated and will most certainly not accrue evenly throughout the years in question. The choice of discount rate (e.g. used in the Net Present Value Method) is subjective, although certain authorities do recommend that the firm's cost of capital should be used. However, one could ask the question 'which cost of capital?'. There are a number of different cost of capital figures which could be used (e.g. current cost; average cost; estimated future cost) and these are subject to different interpretations relating to their calculation. The assessment of risk presents additional problems (e.g. which probability factor to use) and is dependent upon the subjective judgement of the individual.

'The estimated cash flows multiplied by the discount factor make the resultant figures more accurate.' The message to be derived from this apparently absurd statement is that management may become so involved with the method of assessment that they tend to ignore the limitations referred to above. This means that they may in fact be regarding the figures as more accurate than they really are. The information generated from any such assessment can only be as accurate as the original input. Management must therefore appreciate that the financial information is just one small component part of the capital investment decision. Unfortunately accountants cannot foretell the future, e.g. estimated future cash flows will be affected by a multitude of unforeseen factors. The only certainty about the future is the fact that it will be uncertain.

Cash flows can be significantly affected by any trade-in received for the old equipment and the method adopted for financing the project, e.g. HP; leasing etc. This means that for each alternative being considered there could be a number of different cash flow patterns.

The non-financial factors
In addition to the financial aspects of the capital investment decision there are also many other areas which warrant attention such as:

1 *Technical*
    (a) The need for technical superiority.
    (b) Flexibility and adaptability.
    (c) Ease of maintenance.
    (d) Operational considerations, e.g. need to retrain/recruit personnel.
    (e) Servicing arrangements.
    (f) Manuals provided for operating and servicing.
    (g) Peripherals necessary for efficient operation or adding at some future date. It is not unheard of for an organization to purchase equipment and find that they are unable to use it without first buying certain peripherals.
    (h) Capacity.

2 *Imported equipment*
    Exchange rates may affect the position dramatically depending upon the method of payment adopted. An important question which must be answered is 'How good is the supplier's servicing and availability of spares in the UK?' It may be first class in the supplier's own country but very poor in the UK. Other considerations under this heading involve:
    (a) The additional administration necessary to deal with the additional documentation and foreign exchange.
    (b) Delays in delivery of the equipment and spares caused by air and sea transportation problems and political instability.

3 *Size and weight of equipment*
Floors may need strengthening and walls may have to be knocked down and rebuilt to accommodate the equipment. This possibility will affect the cash flows and should not be overlooked.

4 *Standardization of equipment*
The benefits of obtaining similar equipment from a tried and tested supplier can have profound consequences upon the financial analysis. Savings should be possible in the areas of operative training, ease of maintenance and inventory of spares, e.g. one component may fit several different machines.

5 *Look before you buy*
It may well be worth the time and expense to actually inspect the equipment in a working environment. The opportunity to talk with operatives and personnel involved with such equipment should certainly not be neglected.

6 *Human and social factors*
Firms who ignore such factors as safety, noise, fumes etc. in today's complex and diverse business environment do so at their peril. The financial consequences of ignoring them could be catastrophic.

7 *Organizational behaviour*
The effects of 'people problems' upon an organization cannot and should not be underestimated. This area alone could jeopardize the success of the whole venture for reasons such as:
(a) Resistance to change, e.g. introducing new technology.
(b) Empire building, e.g. where sub-unit goals conflict with the organization's own goals.
(c) Perceptions about what the management want.
(d) Organizational structure, e.g. certain personnel may be in control of key information junctions or have direct access to top management.
(e) The boardroom balance of power, e.g. finance versus engineers.

There are, of course, numerous other factors that need to be taken into account, e.g. special offers – two for the price of one; guarantees; and the possibility of renegotiating the terms.

Thus, the so called non-financial factors may have a significant influence upon a firm's long term financial performance and cannot be ignored in the capital investment decision making process.

14

The pricing decision

This chapter consists of a three part package in order to discover the creative aspects of the pricing decision.

The first part of the package reviews the different pricing methods from which a selection has to be made.

The middle section examines a selected sample of the literature relating to pricing, which is particularly relevant to creative cost and management accounting.

The final section takes a look at the making of the pricing decision.

How to cost the right price

In recent years many surveys have been carried out to investigate how business people in general and manufacturers in particular determine the selling prices of their goods and services. Both personal interviews and postal questionnaires invariably produce the same result: the majority of respondents claim that they set their prices by adding some percentage to their costs. However, it is widely known that the concept of cost is rarely free from ambiguity.

The problem with determining the cost is that usually cost per unit depends on the quantity being produced. This is because there are certain fixed costs that must be absorbed over the total production, whatever the level of activity. As the quantity produced increases, the fixed cost per unit decreases. In addition to this, there are the variable costs which are incurred as each unit is produced, which will obviously vary proportionately with production.

This means that the cost of production is not the simple and calculable figure that it is sometimes assumed to be. Worse still, the number of units produced will depend upon demand, and demand itself is influenced by price. So now we have the situation where we are trying to arrive at price with cost as the main determinant, yet cost is itself determined by price.

However, costs do form part of the pricing triad in conjunction with competition and market demand, and as such it is vital that management have detailed knowledge of the ingredients and behaviour of the product costs in order to price products most advantageously within the environment. Although they do not generally determine prices, costs for pricing purposes are essential both for measuring the profit contribution of the selling transaction and as information for comparing different products and services.

Both costs and competition have important roles in pricing strategy. Their relative importance depends on the nature of the industry, the product, and existing market conditions.

There are a number of pricing methods, a number of which are discussed briefly below.

FULL COST PRICING

Research has indicated that in practice some form of full cost pricing or cost plus pricing is frequently employed. By this method, a price is arrived at mainly from the cost side of the equation by adding to variable cost a proportion of the firm's overheads (the proportion being absorbed by each unit depends upon what level of normal output has been established for the year) and then adding to this a percentage mark up for profit.

Selling price = variable cost + fixed cost + % mark up

The obvious advantage of the full cost method is that it assures total recovery of costs. This is particularly important in long-run pricing. Despite its great popularity however, there are definite limitations to full costing as a basis for pricing.

The major criticism of this form of pricing is that:

1   It is impossible in practice to correctly allocate overheads between different products.
2   The total costs of conventional absorption costing are not costs that are good for decision making. Incremental costs are required, i.e. the additional cost which would result from the change in volume.

Establishing a price on the above basis contains dangers in that if these average total costs are regarded as the yardstick for price making, business which is going at a price which is less than total unit cost, but which nevertheless would cover the marginal cost, and make a contribution to fixed costs, may be rejected.

3   It ignores the elasticity of demand. While this rarely can be measured with precision, there are many occasions when a pricing executive can and must predict the effect of a change of price on the quantity sold. Since the full-cost method does not segregate the fixed and variable costs, it is not possible to see what effect a price change will have on profits.
4   The full-cost method fails to give consideration to competition. A business does not operate in a vacuum. Management should not automatically assume that it performs as efficiently as its competitors and treat their lower prices with disdain. Instead, a firm should constantly strive to reduce its costs so that they will be equal to or lower than those of their rivals.
5   The methods do not distinguish between 'out of pocket' and 'sunk' costs. Thus a firm using this method may be inclined to reject orders which do not at the very least cover the total costs involved. However, the acceptance of such orders under certain conditions can increase rather than decrease profits.
6   It applies a flat percentage to the total cost of each product to allow for profit. Executives who use this method invariably state that the profit margin represents a 'fair' return, but they have difficulty in defining what a fair return is without having recourse to other criteria such as invested capital. The method also fails to recognize that all products may not be able to earn the same profit margin.
7   Under the full-cost method no consideration is given to the capital investment required to produce, finance, and distribute individual products or product lines. Yet the real measure of business efficiency is whether a satisfactory return on invested capital is being earned. Failure to

take into account the interest on product-line capital may produce an unbalanced price structure and result in an inefficient recovery of funds to provide for dividends and growth.

However, in practice firms are not blind to consumers' reactions and the fact that a large percentage of firms operate under conditions of oligopoly means that they are extremely aware of the dangers of potential competition in addition to existing competition and therefore set their prices accordingly.

RATE OF RETURN PRICING

A refinement of the basic full cost pricing is the rate of return pricing.

In this method management first decides on a rate of return they would like to achieve in the capital employed. To translate this rate into a percentage mark up on costs, the normal rate of production and its total cost must be estimated, together with the value of the capital employed.

The ratio of normal capital employed to the year's total annual costs is then multiplied by the desired rate of return.

The formula is:

$$\text{Percentage mark up on cost} = \frac{\text{Capital employed}}{\text{Total annual cost}} \times \text{Planned rate of return on capital employed}$$

If any variations occur in the normal rate of output then the planned rate of return will not be achieved.

Rate of return pricing was introduced to relate the mark up to a recognized measurement of profit but the basic problem of allocating the fixed overheads still remains. The refinement is misleading in that the formula gives the mark up a form of credibility which in practice leads to inflexibility in the making of pricing decisions.

BREAK-EVEN ANALYSIS

Break-even analysis is another cost-oriented approach which attempts to use contribution margins in modifying pricing decisions to emphasize the sales volume which must be achieved for the company's product to 'break-even' or achieve some target rate of return.

The distinction between fixed and variable costs depends on a time dimension. In the short run, all costs may be considered fixed. In the long run, all costs may be considered variable because plant output is affected by additions, or the building of new plants, and the investment can be scheduled as a function of anticipated demand. In this sense, expenses for executives, specialists, research, etc. could also be variable, depending on the forecasted demand for the product.

Even when the planning range is restricted to a period of about one year, some costs are semi-fixed, in that new executives may be hired if output goes above a certain figure in the early months, creating higher fixed costs which might have to be borne even if the sales rate later declines. Similarly, although variable costs are typically assumed to be linear, in this kind of analysis such factors as economies of scale, learning curves, quantity discounts, and the like may produce a nonlinear variable cost relationship to output.

MARGINAL COST PRICING

In a highly competitive situation companies may have the opportunity to gain business if they can offer a sufficiently low price. This is especially the case where individual contracts are negotiated, but it is increasingly evident in other industries, the transport industry being no exception. In such a situation the company will no doubt be asking what is the lowest level at which it makes sense to take the business. One approach to this is to carry out a marginal costing calculation.

Previously two types of cost were identified: fixed costs and variable costs. In an industry where demand for the products is elastic, and the ratio of fixed to variable costs is high, it is possible to make a wide range of prices which are all economically possible. In deciding these prices, advocates of marginal cost pricing suggest that fixed costs must be omitted from unit costs and selling prices determined on the basis of marginal cost. A pricing decision involves planning into the future, and as such it should deal solely with the estimated revenues, expenses, and capital outlays. All past outlays are inescapable, 'sunk costs', regardless of how they may be 'costed' for other purposes.

With marginal pricing the firm seeks to fix its prices so as to maximize its total contribution. Unless the manufacturer's products are in direct competition with each other, this objective is achieved by considering each product in isolation and fixing its price at a level which is calculated to maximize total contribution. Marginal pricing has a number of apparent advantages over other cost-based pricing methods:

1 The fact that most firms today operate in a number of markets with multiple products produced by a variety of processes makes the allocation of fixed costs impossible.
2 In many businesses, as technology moves at faster rates, the dominant force is innovation and the long run situation is unpredictable. The situation can develop into a series of short runs and one must aim at maximizing contribution in the short run.
3 It is close to incremental analysis in its choice of costs for decision making (although it neglects opportunity costs which can be very important in the short run decision situation).
4 It can provide better protection against potential competition than prices based on full costs.

Despite the obvious advantages of marginal cost pricing, empirical studies show a widespread use of full cost pricing. Research by John Sizer reveals that many firms use both full cost and marginal cost techniques. Marginal costing appears to be used for what he calls 'secondary' pricing decisions, i.e. tenders, by-products, unusual work, export orders, etc. while full costs usually form the basis of the cost information provided to management for standard products sold in the home market.

It is only when 'normal' output has been achieved or is very likely to be achieved that firms consider accepting orders below their 'normal' average cost of production, or tendering for extra work on prices based on marginal cost.

One must not underestimate the importance of fixed costs; on the contrary, they must be recovered in the long run if the firm is to survive. However, once one has committed resources to their creation then to include them in the analysis of the future can distort the picture. The fear of management is that the emphasis on contribution might lead to accepting business which, although providing a price in excess of marginal costing, uses all the existing excess capacity so that when the opportunity arises to accept high contribution business the firm has no excess capacity.

The biggest drawback to using marginal costing is the problem of forecasting the demand curve. This is also a problem of full cost pricing.

Pricing and decision making

Kaplan (1982) said that:

> If the firm is selling a standard commodity, actively traded in commodity markets, then the firm will almost surely be a price taker, accepting the price given in the marketplace. In this situation the firm may need to determine its scale of operations, its production technology, or whether to be in this market at all, but it will not have to worry about how to set the price. This function will be efficiently carried out in the marketplace.

Problems with the economists' 'profit-maximizing' model are widely recognized: it assumes the demand curve is known; the marginal cost curve is difficult to calculate; many factors influence demand other than price, e.g. quality of sales effort, credit terms offered, etc.

On the other hand, the limitations of cost-plus pricing are equally well known: it ignores demand; the circular reasoning – where unit costs are based on a pre-determined level of activity, which is itself determined by the selling price set; with common fixed costs, the method of arbitrary apportionment will determine price.

Drury (1985) identified the following reasons for using cost-based pricing formulae:

1 To justify prices set because they look 'factual and precise'. Thus a monopolist threatened by public inquiry might reasonably feel that he is safeguarding his case by using cost-plus pricing.
2 To encourage price stability – it may help a firm predict the prices of other firms.
3 Where a firm has so many products it is impossible to calculate a price–volume relationship for them all. A simple pricing method, based on cost, may well be necessary.
4 In response to the main objection that the cost-based pricing formulae ignores demand, it should be noted that the actual price adopted rarely follows the formula without amendment reflecting the current market/economic conditions.

Horngren (1977) said that:

> When used intelligently, the contribution (i.e. marginal costing) approach offers equal or better help than the absorption-costing approach to guiding a pricing decision, because:
> 1 The contribution approach offers more detailed information than the absorption costing approach, because variable and fixed-cost behaviour patterns are delineated.
> 2 A 'normal' or 'target' pricing formula can be as easily developed under the contribution approach as under absorption costing for the 'usual' or 'nonincremental' situations.
> 3 The contribution approach offers an insight into the short-run versus long-run effects of cutting prices on special orders.

He went on to say,

> that it is dangerous to regard either marginal costing or absorption costing as the best guide to pricing decisions. Over-simplification and a lack of understanding and judgement can lead to unprofitable pricing regardless of the kind of costing data available or the cost accounting system used.

In establishing the 'relevant costs' for pricing decisions, Drury emphasized the need to identify the markets being sold into, and whether it was a short or long term decision. Sizer (1976) suggested a price monitoring system. Drury also went on to say:

> When a company produces goods which are tailored specifically to a customer's order, each order will be unique. It will be necessary to estimate the normal annual activity for the production facilities and to calculate a rate per unit of normal activity for charging out the common and unavoidable fixed costs. However, management must be made aware that this rate per unit is appropriate only for a specific level of activity. The actual activity must be monitored against the assumed level, and revised overheads rates calculated if appropriate.
>
> It is essential that the cost information is used in a flexible manner. When the estimated budgeted activity is revised downwards there will be an increase in the overhead charge per unit of activity. It may be incorrect to use the increased overhead charge as a justification for increasing the selling price when activity is declining; a reduction in selling price may be more appropriate.

Horngren concluded re the decision making issue, as:

> The ability to distinguish relevant from irrelevant items and the use of the contribution approach to cost analysis are twin foundations for tackling many decisions. To be relevant to a particular decision, a cost must meet two criteria: (a) it must be an expected 'future' cost; and (b) it must be an element of 'difference' between alternatives. The role that part costs play in decision-making is an auxiliary one. Past (irrelevant) costs are useful because they provide empirical evidence that often helps sharpen 'predictions' of future relevant costs.

Dudick (1985) argued that there are three main methods of product costing and pricing:
1   Conventional methods of product costing and pricing.
2   The return-on-investment method.
3   The marginal contribution method. (See also Appendix G.)
He went on:

> In estimating their costs and selling prices, many (probably most) companies provide for the corporate (and divisional) expenses in the markup factor applied to the product manufacturing cost. This approach, in which an all-encompassing markup percentage is applied, can result in inaccuracies. The reason for this is that there is a built-in assumption that these non-manufacturing expenses are incurred in each product in direct proportion to the manufacturing cost.

He also pointed out that there is no one right way of charging corporate expenses to products. His summary of the advantages of allocating non-manufacturing expenses is reproduced as Appendix H.

The objective of pricing products for sale is to maximize the return on investment. External factors can affect costs and prices as follows:

- The stage of product life cycle.
- Competition within the industry.
- Substitute material.
- Special features of the product.
- Services and assistance to customers.
- Government controls.
- The impact of inflation.

Making the price decision

'It is easy to make a pricing decision. The difficulty comes in attempting to make a price decision that is better than another which could have been selected.' (Alpert)

Earlier on in this chapter we examined the basic pricing approaches, each of which had a degree of suitability in some pricing situation. However, no matter which approach is finally selected, all of them must take into account the fact that the pricing decision takes place in an environment constrained by legal and ethical problems, interrelated demand and costs among products in the product line, relationships with distribution channels, and actions and reactions of competitors. Added to this is the fact that price is influenced by the other controllable variables in a firm's marketing mix, all of which may alter the effectiveness of a particular price in securing profitable sales.

All business decisions require the decision maker to choose between alternative courses of action. This will involve weighing up various costs, revenues, and benefits against each other. It should then be possible to see which decision comes closest to achieving the firm's objectives.

Professor Oxenfeldt has suggested a multi-stage approach to pricing, designed to narrow the range of alternative prices at each successive stage. The stages are as follows: selecting marketing targets; choosing a brand 'image'; composing a marketing mix; selecting a pricing policy; determining a pricing strategy; and arriving at a specific price. It is obvious that these steps are calling for more information than is usually utilized. Information is required regarding the total market, competitive activity, and any relevant government policies, as well as a comprehensive internal information system providing detailed information on costs, revenues and profits.

Once the decision maker has progressed through these stages, he is in a position to consider the remaining pricing alternatives. One must estimate the likely effects of alternative levels of price, revenue, sales volume, selling and promotional expenditures on the following:

1 Within the firm:
   - Costs.
   - Utilization of plant, labour force, etc.
   - Production and inventory levels.
   - Other products and/or total sales.
   - Sources of finance, and cash flow.
2 Outside the firm:
   - Market growth.
   - Market shares.
   - Competitors' performance.
   - Competitors' reactions.

The price setter must then consider the effect of alternating these variables on the following:

1 The overall objectives of the firm.
2 The profit objectives.
3 The market objectives.
4 The other objectives.

The price setter must therefore understand that the selection of a pricing policy involves considering the interests of all of the parties concerned, i.e. other departments in the company, customers (present and potential), competitors, and the government. When all this has been taken into account, the final decision may involve setting price by a process of eliminating alternatives. It should then be possible to see which decision comes closest to achieving the firm's objectives. If after considering all the alternatives, it is decided that none of them will contribute towards the achievement of the objectives, then one should reconsider the product/service specification and design, the revenue, cost and profit variants and the objectives involved.

The number of constraints and variables involved in the pricing situation means that any price decision is certainly going to be a very complex one. With the aid of a computer and suitable program the decision would certainly be made easier; however in the majority of instances the decision maker does not have this resource available and must rely on his or her own evaluative skills. In order to simplify the situation one can look at various parts of the problem 'sequentially' rather than 'simultaneously'. However, in research conducted by the Manchester Business School it was found that decisions made sequentially rather than simultaneously were generally less successful, this being due to the fact that they leave out important component parts of the pricing problem.

Once a decision has been made it is very important that feedback is given on the results of each decision. This involves developing a control system in which operating results are circulated regularly, providing price setters with feedback from their decisions, enabling them to compare the actual and the intended effects of their decisions. This report system should include indicators of performance in terms of sales volume and value, market share, cost, profit and return on assets, and, ideally should be compiled and circulated monthly. Feedback of this sort will provide a way of constantly monitoring changing situations quickly and will provide price setters with a way of reacting quickly to developments in a dynamic way.

Summary

The first section of this chapter reviewed the different pricing methods. Creativity arises from having to make a selection from a number of alternative methods.

Under conditions of uncertainty the full cost approach is attractive to accountants: it provides a starting point from which the process of fixing selling prices can begin.

Full cost pricing may save organizations from accepting orders which would lose money, but it will not save them from losing money through refusing, or failing to obtain orders which would have earned a margin over their incremental cost.

The literature survey covered the views of Kaplan (1982), Drury (1985),

Horngren (1977), Sizer (1976) and Dudick (1985). Kaplan (1982) emphasized the role of the marketplace on the prices of standard commodities.

The reasons for cost-based pricing put forward by Drury (1985) were: to justify prices by giving them a perceived degree of precision; to encourage price stability; and where it is impossible to calculate price–volume relationships.

The contribution (i.e. marginal costing) approach does, according to Horngren, offer more detailed information than the absorption costing approach. It also offers an insight into short-run versus long run outcomes of price reductions on special orders. However, its use can be so over-simplified that it leads to unprofitable pricing.

Dudick (1985) emphasized that the pricing decision cannot ignore external factors.

Drury (1985) also highlighted the need for monitoring the actual level of activity and, if necessary, adjusting the assumed level of activity. The level of activity is a creative variable and most certainly part of cost and management accounting's creative mix.

There are invariably no clear danger signals to indicate when a company has a pricing problem. Only if a regular re-examination of every price (especially to determine whether the original assumptions actually came to pass) is made can one ensure that errors will not continue almost indefinitely. The frequency of such reviews should of course depend upon the nature of the individual market, but prudence dictates that the review be excessively frequent rather than infrequent. Most companies in the past have reviewed their price lists annually, mainly to enable them to take into account any increases in specific costs and to allow for inflation. However, in today's competitive environment, it is appropriate to review prices as frequently as is possible (this does not necessarily involve increasing prices). Price reviews are most commonly instigated to help offset decreasing profit margins, involving a general review of all prices, or, in response to changes in the trading conditions in particular markets for particular products. This is most certainly an area in which management must strive to become more competent.

Price setting must become more sophisticated and take into account a multiplicity of variables. Once set, prices should be subjected to frequent reviews in order to take into account changes in the complex and diverse business environment.

More time, energy, effort and resources must be devoted to making the pricing decision.

Part 5

Conclusions and check lists

15
An evaluation

It has been shown that 'cost' can be defined in many ways, and how various writers have suggested what information is 'relevant' to a particular decision. Belkaoui (1983) pointed out that cost accounting rested not only on accounting but also on organizational, behavioural, and decision making foundations.

This chapter attempts to construct a framework within which the general management of a company can evaluate the costing information it receives, and specify the costing information it requires. It also attempts to identify the practical knowledge/understanding required by the user in order to assess the information provided/requested. Finally it provides a checklist for evaluating costing information and a list of creative cost and management accounting keywords.

Perhaps the evaluation framework developed could be used by researchers to assess the operation of costing systems and the costing information actually provided by cost accountants in different manufacturing companies.

The 'reasonability' of cost-information can be assessed using the framework developed by Kollaritsch (1979) in his 'Elements of requirements of a cost system': Why? What? Accuracy? Who? Time Period? Timing? Form and Mode? A more detailed discussion of these elements is contained in Appendix I.

Why?

The costing information provided must be appropriate to the use made of it. It should reflect the economic, commercial, and manufacturing circumstances faced by the company. Krommer and Muir (1983) supported this contention when they wrote:

> Cost accounting should be the primary barometer of the effectiveness and efficiency of the various operating functions of a company. If used properly, cost accounting is a company's primary operational management information system.

and

> to consider a cost accounting system as something separate and apart from manufacturing and financial systems completely misrepresents what a cost system is.

King (1986) said that changes in manufacturing techniques, manufacturing philosophy, and computers has created problem areas in accounting which include: the cost of quality; the cost justification of factory automation; product costing and pricing; and performance evaluation. Similarly, Giacomino and Doney (1986) stated that:

> Changes in manufacturing evidence focus upon Simplification, Automation, and Integration (SAI) in the manufacturing function, which has many implications for Cost Accounting. The implications of these changes will be seen in the "definition" and "use" of the cost accounting information provided.

The key changes they identified which will impact on the cost accounting systems were:

1 Technological advances: causing manufacturers to become increasingly capital-intensive, and more dependent on 'knowledge workers'. Maintenance costs will become an increasingly larger part of overhead.
2 Shorter product life cycles:
   (a) Performance measures for early stages of product life cycles will be more complex and will require measurements over longer time periods than for measurements of mature products. Facilities for manufacturing new products are less likely to have well-defined measures of performance.
   (b) Measures of performance will have to differ for each stage in the life cycle.
   (c) Overall performance measurement will be difficult in plants producing multiple products at various life cycle stages. The risk is that companies will use efficiency measures for all product lines which are inappropriate for mature products, thus inhibiting the successful introduction of new products.
3 Decreasing labour costs compared with capital-intensive costs. Overhead allocation methods must move away from the emphasis on using direct labour, towards multiple-rate bases. Labour costs are becoming increasingly fixed.
4 Except for materials and energy costs, variable costs will decrease.
5 Increased concern for 'quality costs' will require development of reporting systems incorporating both internal and external sourced data.

On the other hand, the provision of costing-information for stock valuation purposes is well established. In the UK, reasonability must be assessed in the context of SSAP 9. External auditors have a duty to review the reasonability of the stock valuation in coming to an opinion whether or not the accounts offer a 'true and fair view' of a company's performance. A review of five Audit Manuals – Spicer and Pegler (1985); Thomson McLintock (1983); Grant Thornton (1986); Binder Hamlyn (1986); Coopers & Lybrand (1984) – found the common call for 'reasonability and consistency' but all failed to define this, other than via reference to the requirements of SSAP 9. The need to hold a knowledge of the industry, business and organization was, however, recognized.

What?

The costing-information should be relevant to the decision being made, both in respect of the topic and the circumstances faced. The costing-information may be either:
1 A direct product of the costing system.
2 A 'one-off' factor completely external to the costing system, such as for example, an 'opportunity-cost'.

3   A hybrid, where a product of the costing system is adjusted or married with specific circumstances (physical and/or financial) relevant to the costing requirement, and/or a 'one-off' factor.

As circumstances change, there is a need to display creativity in defining what is relevant. However, Claret (1987) raised the question of how accountants can transfer from applying concepts of accuracy, prudence, objectivity and order, into handling risk and uncertainty, committing themselves and their companies, backing their own opinions, being in danger of making mistakes and being held responsible. He asked whether they will be capable of acquiring some of the marketer's personality, such as: outgoing, outward looking, competitive, creative, imaginative, and sensitive to impressions.

Hill and Dimnik (1986) said that the new technologies require the management accountant to play a dual role in their cost-justification:

1   Working with management to establish clear capital budgeting guidelines, e.g. they recommended that management accountants should encourage two modifications to be made to the capital budgeting guidelines:
    (a) Permit the recognition of the value associated with future investment options, (i.e. to give value to qualitative factors) and
    (b) Encourage the downward adjustment of the 'hurdle' (i.e. discount rate) because, for example, products from the flexible manufacturing line can be expected to be of better quality with fewer rejects and recalls.
2   Acting as a gatekeeper in screening proposals to ensure they match the firm's strategic guidelines. With the increasing world-wide competition, organizations can no longer be complacent that 'business will continue as usual'.

Accuracy?

This implies an understanding of:

1   The importance of the cost-information to the problem faced. Should a solution only require knowledge of 'direction' or 'relative cost' etc.? This will affect the required degree of accuracy.
2   The sources of the information. This will include not only the financial data, but also the technical specifications and/or operational environment/assumptions.
3   The relationship between the actual results achieved (as recorded in the costing and/or operational reporting systems), and the standards/estimates used in preparing the costing information.
4   The costing principles followed, and the costing system used.
5   The key factors affecting costs, in terms of cost materiality, and technical specifications.
6   The importance of key accounting considerations, particularly re Balance Sheet values of stock (any write-offs necessary?) and fixed assets (are the outstanding asset lives, as used for depreciation purposes reasonable?).

An important issue within the topic of accuracy is that of 'cost allocation'. Horngren (1977) has said "Beware of full reallocation of actual costs". Where total costs are reallocated on the basis of usage or activity, then a significant change in one department will have a significant and opposite effect on the other departments!

The imperfections of the process of cost allocation/apportionment are obvious. How can one judge whether one suggested cost apportionment is better than an alternative? He went on to say that:

> The whole matter of reallocation is complicated by many computations. There is a misleading aura of precision, which is heightened by elaborate working papers and several decimal places. The choice of a particular method should be influenced by how sensitive the decisions are to the results of the alternative.

He also emphasized cause and effect (whenever ascertainable in an economically justifiable way) as the preferable criterion for cost allocation/apportionment whilst the literature on cost accounting has tended to favour fairness or equity, or benefits received as preferable criteria. Wright (1971) said re the concept of equity as a criterion for cost allocations/apportionments:

> This is a concept which is easy to talk about, harder to write about except in generalities, and very difficult to apply because equity is in the mind of each individual. Yet equity is what this game is all about. Negotiations of contract price are intended to substitute for the automatic equity arising from the armslength bargaining of the market place. The use of accounting in negotiations and settlements should ease the path to an equitable price or settlement.

This statement is a good indication of why creativity exists.

Who?

The user of the information may be internal or external to the organization. The internal user will view the costing information against his specialist knowledge of the company and its operations, and the problem/decision being addressed. Cynically, costing information which supports a pre-determined view, is unlikely to be challenged. That which does not, is likely to be 'questioned' at best, or at worst, rejected out of hand, as 'wrong'. The information provider is then torn between political survival, and the maintenance of professional integrity. A 'way-out' for the information provider is to set out all the assumptions made (both explicit and implicit), and discuss their reasonability with the user. A re-computation based upon the user's assumptions, which should be made quite explicit, would then pass responsibility for the cost information to the user!

In many cases the external user may not have acquired the detailed knowledge necessary to comment upon the costing information provided. He/she must rely upon widely used 'standards', for example, the adoption of SSAP 9 for the valuation of stock – despite the qualifications expressed earlier!

The Cost Accounting Standards Board (CASB) was established by the United States Congress in 1970 to issue cost accounting standards. The purpose of the standards was to achieve uniformity and consistency in the cost accounting practices of defence contractors and subcontractors. In an attempt to accomplish these objectives, the standards dealt with the measurement of costs and the allocation of costs among cost objectives.

Time period

Costing information will always contain an assumption of the time period to which it relates. Inevitably, the longer the future time span to which the data relates, the less certain one can be of its accuracy. Reasonability can only be related to the assumptions made, not to the costing information. However, remember that a series of reasonable assumptions may lead to unreasonable costing information!

Timing

The time and the frequency a report is prepared may provide an insight into the method of its calculation, and thus its reasonableness to the problem/decision being addressed. A frequent report is likely to be a by-product of the formal costing system, and thus based upon the costing principles upon which the costing system has been developed. An infrequent report is more likely to be an ad-hoc report prepared for a specific purpose. The assumptions built into the cost report may, or may not, be appropriate for another problem/decision. A report produced quickly may contain more assumptions which have not been validated, and therefore, the end-product may be less 'reasonable' than if it had been produced at a more leisurely pace – and more comprehensively reviewed.

Form and mode

The form in which the costing information is reported and its mode of conveyance may impact on its reasonability via:

- The comparisons it draws with other pieces of cost data, such as budgeted, forecasted, or 'actual' data.
- The level of detail provided – including a statement of the assumptions made.
- The impact on the receiver – a verbal presentation as distinct from a written document, is likely to have a greater impact on the information receiver.

Conclusion

The reasonability of costing information could be assessed in terms of:

1 The costing principles followed in preparing the information and their relevance to the problem/decision being addressed.
2 The assumptions (explicit and implicit) upon which the information is based.
3 The sources of information – financial and technical – which are used in calculating 'cost' and its 'accuracy' relative to the accuracy requirement.
4 Its presentation.

A 'costing' financial model

A costing financial model is a model of the company based upon the structure, classifications, and assumptions built into the company's costing system. It will be inter-related to the company's financial accounts. Krommer and Muir (1983) said that the cost accounting system should:

1 Link with the total costs provided by the different feeder accounting procedures.
2 Provide timely, accurate and complete information about the critical success factors of the company's business.
3 Be integrated with reliable and controlled operational systems for inventory, production and project management planning and control.

Different authors have suggested different steps in developing a cost system. For example, Rotch and others (1982) suggested:

1 Determining goals and objectives of the company.
2 Identifying organizational constraints.
3 Identifying key success variables for each responsibility centre.
4 Applying evaluation criteria. Evaluation may include some or all of the following criteria:
   (a) Goal congruence.
   (b) Feasibility.
   (c) Controllability.
   (d) Understandability.
   (e) Fairness.
   (f) Long run/short run balance.
5 Testing and recommending change.

A more practical and detailed list of tasks is shown in Appendix J.

The above emphasizes the need to understand the company's operational environment and the key 'success variables'. In discussing a consulting engagement to design a new production system, Seglund and Iberrache (1984) provided a two stage approach to designing a responsive system.

Stage 1: General steps:
● Analyse the accounting system.
● Determine desired measures of performance.
● Select a production activity to serve as a benchmark for measuring project success.

Stage 2: Specific steps:
● Determine whether a job order, process cost, or a hybrid system is appropriate.
● Identify key variables to be measured and prepare document flow charts.
● Propose placing data on a computer system compatible with current operations.

A flow diagram of the cost accounting process is shown in Appendix K. This diagram typifies a 'full cost' system.

The costing financial model should incorporate the key success variables – and the factors (financial and physical/technical) which influence them. These should include those key aspects of strategy and policy which have been identified in the company's Corporate Plan. The model should be used to monitor 'actual results' against the major assumptions built into the costing system, and the costing information provided. This will provide a basis upon which to assess the 'reasonableness' of the information provided.

The advantages to general management from such a model are:

1 Costing information is reconcilable to, and consistent with, the company's declared results and plans/budgets/forecasts.
2 Simplicity of presentation.
3 A basis to assess 'reasonableness' of costing information produced routinely, particularly in respect of 'accuracy', 'production activity' and 'cost behaviour'.
4 An up-to-date monitoring of the company's key success variables.
5 An integration of financial and physical/technical factors, facilitating the interpretation of information between the different functional activities.

A checklist for evaluating costing information

To gain the most benefit from sophisticated cost accounting systems, management should keep in mind two significant principles:

1 Cost accounting should provide information measuring the utilization of resources and the impact of anticipated changes to those resources.
2 Cost accounting is not an isolated system. It is the proper merging of financial, administrative, and operational planning and control systems. The data produced from any cost accounting process is only as comprehensive, timely, or accurate as the information given it by the operational and administrative support feeder systems.

This checklist is intended for use by general management in order to assess the costing information they receive and/or the costing information they request. It is inevitable that a generalized checklist such as this will not cater for all circumstances. It is, therefore, recommended that the user refines the checklist from their own personal experience of the environment/costing systems with which they are involved.

A comprehensive checklist of typical cost information required is shown in Appendix L.

Checklist

1 To what use is the costing-information to be put?
2 What 'costs' are relevant to the decision:
   (a) Variable – over what range of activity?
             – are they 'naturally' variable, or is management action required?
   (b) Incremental – over what time period?
3 How significant is the costing information to the decision? Is the 'absolute' or 'relative' cost important? How 'accurate' does the costing information have to be?
4 What type of costing system is operated by the company?
   (a) Standard.
   (b) Actual.
   (c) Process costing.
   (d) Job costing.
   (e) What combination of the above is used?

5   How are 'costs' defined within the costing system?
    (a) Direct (material and direct labour only).
    (b) Variable (direct + variable manufacturing overheads).
    (c) Full-manufacturing costs.
    (d) Are administration and selling costs allocated to products, and/or activities?
6   If costs include allocations, are they based on Horngren's (1977) suggested guidelines? For example:
    (a) Plan and control the costs of service departments or divisions just like those of operating departments or divisions. The fundamental distinctions between variable and fixed cost behaviour should be preserved. Where feasible, use flexible budgets and standards, not static budgets and standards.
    (b) Where feasible, use a dual system that distinguishes between variable and fixed costs.
    (c) To charge departments, use predetermined or budgeted unit prices or rates, not actual unit prices or rates.
    (d) Where feasible, in addition to using predetermined prices, charge on the basis of predetermined standard or budgeted efficiency allowed for services rendered.
    (e) Do not allow short-run charges to a specific department to depend on how much of the service is being consumed by other departments.
7   If the 'costs' are to be used for pricing purposes, are they based on Dudick's (1985) recommendations? For example:
    (a) Overhead rates should identify the variable and fixed segments to facilitate profit volume analyses.
    (b) Nonmanufacturing (corporate) costs such as selling, general administration, and research and development must also be included in cost estimates for cost/price comparisons.
    (c) Cost estimates should include a provision for production losses. An across-the-board measure is acceptable for products that are homogeneous.
    (d) Costs used in estimating should be current. They should reflect current prices, current labour rates, and current manufacturing procedures.
    (e) If cost estimates are being prepared for pricing an order to be delivered, say, six months hence, they should reflect the anticipated costs at that time.
    (f) Cost estimates should provide sufficient information, such as set-up costs, to facilitate the determination of unit costs for various quantities to be priced.
8   Is the company facing any of the six major problems of cost estimating as identified by Dudick?, namely:
    (a) Insufficient lead time to prepare the estimate – necessary to spell out the assumptions made.
    (b) Cost estimates either too high or too low – this may be due to:
        • excessive contingency provisions
        • differences in manufacturing process between products not properly taken into account, e.g. plant wide overhead rate used
    (c) Costing procedure not correlated with current production facilities.
    (d) Operating personnel not consulted, e.g. may lead to inappropriate bases for apportioning overheads etc.
    (e) Size of order not definite – small orders may not bear the full cost of setup.
    (f) Poor feedback – little or no feedback on actual costs compared with the original estimate.

9   Are the assumptions made in preparing the cost information identified explicitly?
10 What are the sources of the information used and/or the assumptions adopted?
    (a) Financial:
        • material price(s)
        • definition of direct material (types)
        • definition of direct labour (operations and cost elements)
        • direct labour rate(s)
        • labour utilization/idle time
        • variable and fixed overhead rates (are they company-wide or cost centre/department based?)
        • production capacity for budgeted level of overheads
    (b) Technical:
        • material requirements
        • scrap/wastage rates
        • manufacturing route(s)
        • direct labour times/labour grades
        • machine/labour efficiencies/performances
        • capacity utilization
11 Is the above information monitored? By whom? How? Is the 'feedback' incorporated into the costing system on a regular basis? That is, if 'standards' are used, how often are they up-dated?
12 Does the company have internal auditors? Baxendale and Melton (1982) suggested that audit procedures related to cost accounting standards should be incorporated into the areas upon which internal auditing traditionally focuses, namely:
    (a) Disclosure statement.
    (b) Property accounting.
    (c) Unallowable costs.
    (d) Allocation of costs: the authors suggest that the auditors can,

    examine the reasonableness of the process by which costs are allocated from the department to intermediate cost objectives and then ultimately to final cost objectives, without suggesting any tests of reasonability!

13 In identifying fixed and variable costs, are Dudick's guidelines followed? For example:
    (a) The chart of accounts should not be structured to break down the natural expenses by their fixed and variable segments.
    (b) Cost behaviour of a natural expense item can change with the application. Electricity, for example, is highly variable when used for operating motors. But when used for heating annealing furnaces, it will be highly fixed.
    (c) In an automated operation in which one operator operates two or more machines, direct labour can behave as a fixed cost when volume drops because the operator will still be needed even when some of the machines have been idle.
    (d) Inflation (or deflation) can affect cost behaviour because costs can be affected by price changes even though the level of activity, as measured by labour hours or machine hours, remains relatively stable.
    (e) Don't rely on mathematical formulae for determining cost behaviour. The determination of cost behaviour, and under what conditions behaviour

changes, can only be determined by knowing the business and the nature of the manufacturing (or service) operations.

14 Does the cost report (and mode) emphasize *why* there is a cost, not just *where* it is? That is, is Woodward's (1986) 'causal costing' being practised?

15 Does the costing information distinguish between that which is a product of:
(a) The routine/formal costing system?
(b) An ad hoc study by the cost accountant?
(c) The 'valuation' of qualitative data?

Keywords

The cost and management 'creative mix' or 'creativity portfolio' consists of:

behavioural aspects – in particular the role of 'gatekeeper'.

concepts – the application of accounting concepts.

historic cost – looks backwards not forwards.

innocent creativity – the failure to appreciate limitations. The failure to monitor and review at frequent intervals, e.g. basic assumptions in budgeting. Errors, e.g. the denomination of quantity in stock taking.

myths – the fact that certain costs are calculated gives them a perception of accuracy and an air of respectability. Examiners and textbook writers may promote misleading myths, e.g. apportioning costs which in a real world situation could be allocated.

objectives – the setting of cost objectives.

oversimplifications – e.g. when a multi-variable approach is called for.

perceptions – e.g. of managerial objectives and user needs. Also perceptions about the business environment.

predetermination – costs, revenues, standards, levels of activity, targets and basic assumptions have to be predetermined in budgeting/standard costing systems. Predetermined figures are only estimates.

pricing – e.g. transfer pricing.

Statements of Standard Accounting Practice – involve quite a lot of choice, e.g. SSAP 9 Stocks and Work-in-Progress. May be ignored when it comes to providing information for internal reporting purposes.

subjective judgement – numerous choices between alternatives have to be made. Qualitative factors have to be assessed, e.g. non-financial factors. Decisions have to be taken on how costs are to be analysed, e.g. idle time.

terminology – lots of the terms used in cost and management accountancy are extremely difficult to define, e.g.

Normal activity

Relevant cost

Direct labour

Cost may be classified in many different ways.

users – the needs of the user can affect the way in which costs are computed, e.g. figures prepared by a trade union and figures prepared by the employers.

valuation – of stocks of raw materials, work-in-progress, finished goods and other assets. The use of derived stock figures in periodic statements. The valuation of by-products and joint products in process costing at the point of separation. Long term contracts. The 'cut off procedure'.

window dressing – SO, BEWARE OF ACCOUNTANTS!

Appendices

Appendix A

STANDARDS OF ETHICAL CONDUCT FOR MANAGEMENT
ACCOUNTANTS

Competence

Management accountants have a responsibility to:
- Maintain an appropriate level of professional competence by ongoing development of their knowledge and skills.
- Perform their professional duties in accordance with relevant laws, regulations, and technical standards.
- Prepare complete and clear reports and recommendations after appropriate analyses of relevant and reliable information.

Confidentiality

Management accountants have a responsibility to:
- Refrain from disclosing confidential information acquired in the course of their work except when authorized, unless legally obligated to do so.
- Inform subordinates as appropriate regarding the confidentiality of information acquired in the course of their work and monitor their activities to assure the maintenance of that confidentiality.
- Refrain from using or appearing to use confidential information acquired in the course of their work for unethical or illegal advantage either personally or through third parties.

Integrity

Management accountants have a responsibility to:
- Avoid actual or apparent conflicts of interest and advise all appropriate parties of any potential conflict.
- Refrain from engaging in any activity that would prejudice their ability to carry out their duties ethically.
- Refuse any gift, favour, or hospitality that would influence or would appear to influence their actions.

- Refrain from either actively or passively subverting the attainment of the organization's legitimate and ethical objectives.
- Recognize and communicate professional limitations or other constraints that preclude responsible judgement or successful performance of an activity.
- Communicate unfavourable as well as favourable information and professional judgements or opinions.
- Refrain from engaging in or supporting any activity that would discredit the profession.

Objectivity

Management accountants have a responsibility to:
- Communicate information fairly and objectively.
- Disclose fully all relevant information that could reasonably be expected to influence an intended user's understanding of the reports, comments, and recommendations presented.

Reprinted by permission of The National Association of Accountants, Statement on Management Accounting, No. 1C, 1 June, 1983.

Appendix B

SURVEY OF MANUFACTURING COSTS

Dudick selected a company from different industries to demonstrate the significance of manufacturing costs, and its variability between different industries.

Manufacturing cost significance by industries

	(a) Manufacturing cost of sales %	(b) R & D, Marketing and Administration %	Operating Income %	Total %
Cosmetics	37	46	17	100
Word-Processing Equipment	44	43	13	100
Pharmaceuticals	45	42	13	100
Consumer Products	72	21	7	100
Industrial Valves	74	20	6	100
Motor Vehicles				
1980	97	5	(2)	100
1979	89	4	7	100

(a) Includes depreciation and amortization of tools, where applicable.
(b) This was combined because all companies did not break these figures down.

He also provided an analysis of the makeup of manufacturing cost for 6 companies (shown below), so as to indicate that the cost accounting needs of the different types of companies would vary.

	Highly labour paced	Automatic equipment highly machine paced	Product with high material content	Composite of six companies
	(3 companies)	(1 company)	(2 companies)	
Direct material	30	59	72	62
Direct labour	24	5	8	13
Overhead	46	36	20	25
Manufacturing cost	100%	100%	100%	100%

Breakdown of overheads

Indirect labour and fringe benefits	60	47	65	45
Maintenance labour and repair material	7	17	4	14
Depreciation	5	12	4	13
Occupancy costs	6	7	10	6
All other (a)	22	17	17	22
Total Overhead	100%	100%	100%	100%
Number of items in (a)	26	23	18	16

Source: Thomas S. Dudick, *Dudick on Manufacturing Cost Controls* (Englewood Cliffs, N.J., Prentice-Hall Inc., 1985). Reprinted by permission of Simon Schuster.

Appendix C

ALLOCATING CENTRAL SERVICES EXPENSES

The author contends that where a branch manager has no control over the central administration costs, and therefore no opportunity to reduce the costs charged to the branch, cost allocation is an 'exercise in number juggling'. However, when an operating department controls its use of a centrally provided service, and therefore influences the central service's costs, an allocation charge is appropriate.

Unfortunately the most common method of cost allocation (i.e. 100% recharging on basis of usage) can have a counter-productive effect on managerial behaviour. *Ceterus paribus*, the reduced usage by a department will reduce its total allocation, but its cost per unit of usage will have increased! To avoid this type of problem the author suggests using the following allocation rules:

- When the demand for a service is well below its capacity, the allocation charge should be the service's variable cost.
- As demand for the service rises towards the service's capacity, the allocation charge should rise toward 'full-cost'.
- If demand for the service should exceed the service's capacity, the allocation charge should be increased, even beyond full cost, until the demand is reduced to the service's capacity.

These suggested allocation rules are appropriate only when the service has no external market. In these cases the following rules should be followed:

- The allocation charge should always be less than or equal to the price at which the service can be purchased from other firms.
- The allocation charge should never be less than the prices at which your firm could sell the service to other firms.

The object of allocation charges is to guide operating department managers to use a centrally provided service efficiently. When a department manager chooses to use the amount of centrally provided services which increases the departmental income, the total firm's income will simultaneously be increased.

Source: L. B. Hoshower, 'Appropriate allocation: "free-market" billing makes best use of internal services', *Management World* (USA), October 1983, pp. 32–36.
Reprinted by permission of Management World (USA) Administrative Management Society.

Appendix D

DIRECT COSTING VERSUS FULL COSTING

Features of the systems	*Direct costing*	*Full costing*
Income statements	Easier for non-accounting operating personnel to understand.	Complicated by effect of over- and under-absorbed overhead on reported profit.
Difference in reported profit by the two methods	Profits vary with changes in sales volume.	Profits vary with production volume rather than with sales volume.
Inventory valuation	Inventory value excludes fixed costs and therefore understates the value of the inventory.	Inventory value includes fixed costs and is therefore fully valued.
Product costs	Product cost understates the true product cost.	Products are fully costed.
Product pricing	Understatement of product costs could result in underpriced products.	Full costing would reduce the possibility of underpricing.
Analytical features:		
• Break even sales volume	Facilitates calculation of break even sales volume based on monthly income statement.	Cannot be calculated without knowledge of variable and fixed costs.
• Make–buy decisions	Facilitates determination of economics of making the product in-house versus purchasing on the outside.	Cannot be calculated without knowledge of variable and fixed costs.
• Product mix changes	Effect of profits of product mix changes is facilitated through availability of variable and fixed cost breakdown.	Cannot be calculated without knowledge of fixed and variable costs.

| Variable and fixed cost breakdown | Incorrect determination of variable and fixed costs can impair accuracy of the system. | Not a problem since variable and fixed costs are not identified. |
| Legality of cost system | Can be used for internal analysis and reporting but not for external reporting. | Treasury department and SEC* mandates use full costing for external reporting. |

* This is a US publication – the UK equivalents could be the Inland Revenue, and SSAP 9 together with the Stock Exchange Rule Book.

Source: Thomas S. Dudick, *Dudick on Manufacturing Cost Controls* (Englewood Cliffs, N.J., Prentice-Hall Inc., 1985). Reprinted by permission of Simon Schuster.

Appendix E

ADVANTAGES AND DISADVANTAGES OF JOB AND PROCESS COSTING SYSTEMS

Job costing

Advantages
1 Results in more accurate costing because it 'customizes' the costing to reflect the differences in the various jobs.
2 The cost of each job can be directly associated with the resulting sales price.
3 Costs of products can be compared with the original estimate on which the selling price was based.
4 The profitability of each job can be quickly determined.
5 Inventory control will be more reliable because the inventory will be identified separately for each job. As the job is completed and shipped, the inventory will be decreased. This should reduce the physical to book differences so characteristic of process costing.
6 The detailed information for the various jobs will be useful in future estimating.

Disadvantages
1 Requires a great deal more work than process costing because of the greater detail of posting costs to individual jobs rather than to departments.
2 Highly engineered jobs frequently must be supported by a great deal of documentation. This type of cost is difficult to estimate in advance.
3 The practice of 'borrowing' parts from one job to be used on another can greatly distort the costing procedures when paperwork adjustments are ignored – as they frequently are.

Process costing

Advantages
1 Process costing is simpler.
2 Not necessary to accumulate costs for many individual orders; costs are accumulated by department.
3 Availability of departmental costs facilitates responsibility reporting.
4 Standardized nature of products facilitates measurement of productivity.

5 Repetitiveness of production permits establishment of standards for determination of variations from standard cost.

Disadvantages
1 Profitability by customer order is not practical to compute.
2 Inventory more difficult to control because of greater number of parts and subassemblies in process. Physical to book inventory differences more likely in process costing.

Source: Thomas S. Dudick, *Dudick on Manufacturing Cost Controls.* (Englewood Cliffs, N.J. Prentice-Hall Inc., 1985.) Reprinted by permission of Simon Schuster.

Appendix F

JOINT AND BY-PRODUCT COSTING

Joint product and by-product costing arise in situations where the production of one product makes inevitable the production of other products. If the sales value of the different products are significant, then they are referred to as 'joint-products', but if the sales value of one product is not significant, then it is referred to as a by-product. The different products are not identifiable as different individual products until the 'split-off' point in the production process. The 'cost' of the joint or by-product at the 'split-off' point can be considered its material cost.

There are various methods of apportioning joint costs to joint products, but there are two basic categories:

1 Those based on 'physical measures' such as weight, volume etc. These bear no relationship to 'market value', therefore one may attribute 'cost' higher than sales value! A further problem may arise from the need for a common unit of measurement where, for example, products might consist of solids, liquids, and gases. In these instances, conversion tables will be necessary with their inevitable built in assumptions.
2 Those based on 'market values' of the products. In practice it is likely that joint products will be processed beyond the 'split-off' point, so it is necessary to apportion costs on the basis of the 'net realizable value', i.e. sales value less additional costs past the split-off point.

Cats-Baril and others (1986) pointed out that there are cases where jointness exists among products in terms of other, less obvious, attributes. Typically, in these situations, the products have not been viewed as joint for costing purposes. For example, in the semiconductor industry, the production of memory chips of differential quality represents such a case, because the output consists of different quality 'chips' from a common production run.

They argued that the choice between allocating joint costs on a 'physical' or 'market value' basis is arbitrary when the proportions of the joint products composing the output mix are fixed and cannot be changed. However the choice is not arbitrary if the proportions can be varied and there is a relationship between the total cost and the total value of the output. The author contends that in the latter instance, a market value approach to joint cost allocation is the most rational approach.

The limitations of joint cost allocations for decision-making are widely recognized.

Drury (1985), said that 'Joint product costs calculated for stock valuation are entirely inappropriate for decision-making. For short-term decision-making "relevant costs" should be used – these represent the additional costs which a product incurs, or those costs which will be eliminated if the product is not made. Consequently, joint cost allocations should not be used when making short-term decisions as they are expected to remain unchanged in the short run.'

Written by Michael Magin.

Appendix G

KEY FEATURES OF THREE METHODS OF COST ESTIMATING

Cost estimate methods	*Advantages*	*Disadvantages*
Conventional method: applies a markup percentage to total manufacturing cost to arrive at the selling price which includes selling and administrative expenses.	Cost buildup follows steps in the same sequence in which the product is manufactured. It shows the types of material, quantity required, and cost. Also shown are the manufacturing operations, cost of labour, and overhead and allowances for production losses.	Most companies apply the same markup percentage to material and conversion cost.
Return on investment: these do not include selling and administrative expenses which are added separately.	Manufacturing-related investments are identified as those that relate to conversion costs. Separate markup percentages are then applied to material and to conversion costs.	If some operations require high investment in equipment and others require a small investment, it may be necessary to develop a number of markup percentages to accommodate various combinations of operations on different products.
Marginal contribution: these do not include selling and administrative expenses which are added separately.	Availability of profit contribution percentages by products identifies individual product profitability. This can be useful in lowering the price of private brands	Tends to depress selling prices because many companies use this method for the purpose of 'shaving' fixed costs.

when the brand products
absorb their full measure
of fixed costs.

Source: Thomas S. Dudick, *Dudick on Manufacturing Cost Controls* p. 252 (Englewood Cliffs N.J. Prentice-Hall Inc., 1985). Reprinted by permission of Simon Schuster.

Appendix H

ALLOCATING NON MANUFACTURING COSTS BY SALES
CATEGORIES

Allocation method	*Advantages*	*Disadvantages*
Include nonmanufacturing costs in markup percentage applied to manufacturing costs.	Simplifies allocation.	Assumes that nonmanufacturing costs vary directly with manufacturing costs.
Include nonmanufacturing costs in markup percentage applied to direct labour and overhead only (conversion cost).	Excludes the influence of variations in material content of the various products.	Assumes that nonmanufacturing costs will always vary with conversion costs.
Allocate nonmanufacturing costs to products on the basis of sales volume; minor products charged a small fixed fee representing a 'readiness-to-serve' cost.	Avoids penalizing small volume products that permit the company to utilize idle time of the equipment during off-peak periods.	Allocation on basis of sales may not reflect nonmanufacturing costs incurred on individual products.
'Interest rate' method applied to each plant on the basis of the plant's investment in inventory and net fixed assets. Interest rate calculated by dividing total nonmanufacturing costs by factory investment.	Provides incentive to individual factories to maintain minimal investments consistent with production requirements.	Incurrence of nonmanufacturing costs may not always be directly related to factory investment.
Allocate nonmanufacturing costs to categories of sales on the basis of services rendered.	Recognizes incurrence of certain nonmanufacturing costs, such as those required for export sales, sales to distributors, and selling direct to customers	Not useful in companies that fabricate parts and subassemblies in some plants and assemble the finished product in others.

through company sales
force.

Source: Thomas S. Dudick, *Dudick on Manufacturing Cost Controls* p. 259 (Englewood Cliffs, N.J., Prentice-Hall Inc., 1985). Reprinted by permission of Simon Schuster.

Appendix I

ELEMENTS OF REQUIREMENTS OF A COST SYSTEM

Why?
Objectives of the system or purposes for which information is required

What?
Three facets of information:

1   Transactions or results.
2   Business segment to which they pertain.
3   Methods and techniques of reporting.

Who?
Who is the user?
  External:
  ● agency, etc.
  ● statute, if any
  Internal:
  ● department
  ● title
Time period
Time period covered by report
Timing
● By what time report is required
● Frequency of reporting
Accuracy
Desired degree of accuracy of information
Form and mode
● Form of reporting information
● Mode of conveying report

Reprinted by permission of Publishing Horizons, Inc. From *Cost Concepts for Planning, Decisions and Controls: Concepts and Techniques* by Felix P. Kollaritsch.

Appendix J

BUILDING BLOCKS OF COST SYSTEM DESIGN AND IMPLEMENTATION

Stage 1: System analysis

Steps
● Define objectives and scope of the cost system.
● Gain understanding of the company and its business.
● Determine cost information needs.

Stage 2: System design

Steps
- Make a cost system feasibility study and outline.
- Design common aspects of a cost control system.
- Select cost methods.
- Establish responsibility centres and cost centres.
- Design a direct material cost system.
- Design a direct labour cost system.
- Design a manufacturing overhead cost system.
- Design marketing and administrative cost systems.
- Design cost reports.
- Design cost records and procedures.
- Develop a chart of accounts.

Stage 3: System implementation

Steps
- Synthesize and test the system.
- Present and sell the system to users.
- Implement, operate, refine, maintain, and revise the system.
- Prepare a systems manual.

Reprinted by permission of Publishing Horizons, Inc. From *Cost Concepts for Planning, Decisions, and Controls: Concepts and Techniques* by Felix P. Kollaritsch.

Appendix K

FLOW DIAGRAM OF THE COST ACCOUNTING PROCESS

See page 155.

Appendix L

CHECKLIST OF TYPICAL COST INFORMATION REQUIRED

1   Capacity and production

Capacity
    Theoretical
    Practical
    Normal
    Actual utilized
    Overutilization or under-utilization of capacity compared with planned utilization

Machine efficiency (production ÷ machine hours)
    Actual
    Standard or expected
    Variances from standard or expected efficiency

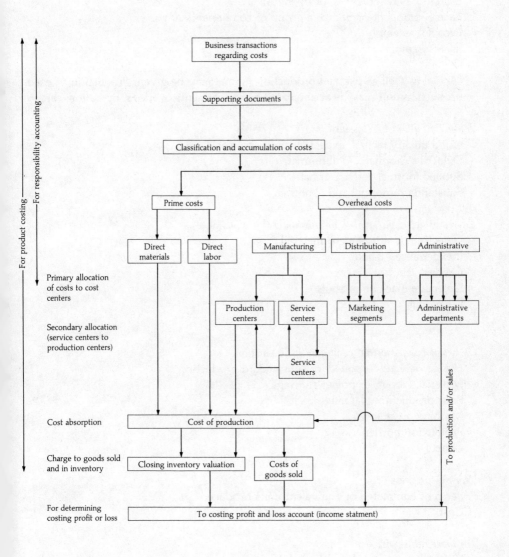

Fig A1   Flow diagram of cost accounting process

Reprinted by permission of Publishing Horizons, Inc. From *Cost Concepts for Planning, Decisions, and Controls: Concepts and Techniques* by Felix P. Kollaritsch.

Production of each production unit, which may be one or more of the following:
    Each product
    Each group of products
    Each job, batch, process, or operation
    Each component or part of a group of components or parts
    Each subassembly
    Each assembly
    Others
    (Actual as well as planned production figures may be given. Production of each
    production unit may be accumulated by departments, workers, operations, etc.)

Production quantity, classified into:
    Good quality (actual, expected, and variance)
    Defective (normal and abnormal)
    Spoiled (normal and abnormal)
    Substandard (normal and abnormal)

Causes of defective, spoiled, or substandard production
    Defective or substandard material
    Inexperienced labour
    Careless labour
    Defective machine or tools
    Power cut
    Others

Causes of below-normal good quality production
    Higher defective, spoiled, or substandard production
    Material, labour, or power shortage
    Poor production planning
    Machine breakdown
    Production bottleneck
    Others

Work in progress
    Per cent completed or equivalent units produced
    Cost

Turnover ratios, etc.
    Finished goods produced ÷ work in process
    Length of production cycle
    Length of each process, operation, or job cycle

2 Product cost information

Total and unit costs of each of the production units. Total and unit costs may be
broken down into cost elements, major cost elements, or the appropriate classification
of various cost elements (e.g. direct materials, direct labour, and manufacturing
overhead; variable and fixed costs; etc.)

3 Direct materials

The following information concerning direct materials may be required (a) in total for *all* direct materials or separately for each material or a *group* of materials or only for significant items of material; (b) in total for *all* production units or separately for *each* production unit:

Consumption and cost (in quantitative and monetary terms)
    Actual
    Variance from standard or estimated consumption and cost:
        Price variance and quantity variance

Yield (production ÷ consumption)
    Actual
    Variance from standard or estimated yield

Causes of variance in consumption and yield
    Defective material
    Improper specifications
    Substandard or superior materials
    Improper mix of materials
    Substandard or superior labour
    Inadequate training
    Faulty workmanship
    Machine breakdown or defect
    Power cut
    Production interruption due to material, labour, or power shortage
    Old standards
    Material loss or gain
    Others

Material losses (in quantitative and monetary terms)
    Scrap (normal and abnormal)
    Waste (normal and abnormal)
    Natural loss or gain due to shrinkage, evaporation, etc. (normal and abnormal)

Damage, deterioration, theft, etc. during transit, storage in stockroom, or material handling in factory
    Defective material
    Obsolete material
    Slow-moving material (aging analysis)
    Ratios (in quantitative and monetary terms)
        Material consumed ÷ material consumption
        Material loss ÷ good production
    Material requirements (monthly, weekly, etc.)
    Material on hand

4 Direct labour

The following information concerning direct labour may be required:
(a) In total for all direct workers or separately for each worker or a group of workers,

(b) In total for all production units or separately for each production unit or a group of production units,

(c) For the company as a whole and separately for each department or division

Availability (required or actually available)
    Number of direct workers
    Number of direct person-hours or person-days
    Both classified into:
        Permanent and temporary
        Skilled and unskilled

Direct labour cost
    Total
    Breakdown by cost elements, e.g.:
        Wages on time basis
        Bonus or incentive payments
        Piece-rate payments
        Normal and overtime payments
        Fringe benefits (e.g. payroll taxes, pensions, etc.)
        Comparison with predetermined costs
    Classified into:
        Payments to permanent and temporary workers
        Payments to skilled and unskilled workers
    Average hourly or daily rate

Labour utilization and idle time (in terms of time and cost)
    Actual productive and idle time
    Variances from standard or estimate, i.e. normal and abnormal idle time
    Utilization and idle time may be expressed as a percentage of total time or cost paid
    Cost and causes of idle time
        Causes:
            Waiting for work
            Waiting for instructions
            Waiting for fellow workers
            Lack of material
            Machine breakdown
            Waiting for machine and tools
            Others

Labour efficiency (production ÷ labour time or cost)
    Actual
    Variance from standard or estimate

Causes of labour efficiency variances
    Excess or lack of workers
    Inefficient or superior labour
    Trainees or new workers
    Improper or better supervision
    Defective or superior material
    Defective or superior machine or tools

Go slow action by workers
Improper or better production scheduling or better plant layout
Outdated standards
Other (e.g. absenteeism due to bad weather, flood, etc.)

Miscellaneous
Labour turnover rate
Cost of labour turnover (with details; e.g. costs of hiring, training, production losses, etc.)
Causes of labour turnover
Absenteeism rate
Others

5   Manufacturing overhead costs

The following information in total and separately for each cost centre and responsibility centre:

Cost of each of the cost elements or a group of them
Indirect material (quantity and cost)
Indirect labour (time or number of employees and cost), with breakdown into managerial, supervisory, etc.
Other expenses, with classification by nature of expenses
Only actual cost figures
Actual, budgeted or estimated, and variances
   Budgets may be based on standard costs and may be fixed or flexible
   Causes of variances
Classification of each cost item by controllability, i.e. separation of controllable and noncontrollable costs
Classification of each cost element by behaviour, i.e. separation of fixed, variable, and semivariable costs
Overhead cost absorption rates
   Actual or predetermined overhead cost per production unit

6   Sales

The following information separately for each product or a group of products:

Sales (quantity, price, and total amount)
Actual
Comparison with budgets or goals
Variances

Analysis of sales variance
Quantity
Price
Product mix

Ratios
Sales turnover ratio (to reveal slow-moving products, excessive inventory, or inadequate inventory) = sales ÷ finished goods inventory

7 Distribution expenses

Classification of expenses by nature,
   e.g. salaries, advertisement, travelling, etc.

Classification of expenses by functions,
   e.g. warehousing, advertising, order-getting, order filling, billing, etc.

Each of the above classifications of expenses identified with segments and methods of marketing, as for example:
   Territories
   Products or groups of products (in total and per unit of product sold)
   Customers or types of customers
   Sales channels
   Sales representatives
   Methods of distribution
   Size of orders (to determine economic order size, charge extra cost for smaller orders, or give discount for larger orders)
   Special orders
   Terms of sale (cash or credit, different credit periods, etc.)

For cost control, the above data are identified with persons responsible
   Only actual cost figures
   Actual, budgeted, variances
     Budget may be fixed or flexible
     Causes of variances

Each cost element may be classified into fixed, semifixed, and variable categories

8 General and administrative expenses

Classification of expenses by
   Nature, e.g. salaries, donations, audit fees, etc.
   Functions, e.g. accounting, finance, legal, secretarial, personnel, etc.

Only actual cost figures or
   Actual, budgeted and variances. Usually, administrative expenses are controlled through a fixed budget

9 Profitability

Profit for the company as a whole classified by profit centres, which may be:
   Divisions
   Products or product groups
   Territories
   Customers
   Channels of sales
   Channels of distribution
   Sales representatives
   Others

Profit may be computed on:
(a) Total cost basis or direct cost basis, i.e. on contribution margin approach

(b) Actual or standard cost method. Actual profits may be compared with budgeted profits or actual profits of past period

Profit margin may be expressed as:
    Gross profit on sales (in total, per unit, and as a percentage of sales or cost of goods sold)
    Operating income on sales (in total, per unit, and as a percentage of sales or cost of goods sold)
    Profit per unit of key or limiting factor (e.g. profit by products, per machine hour, per unit of direct material in short supply, etc.)

10   Inventory and purchases

Quantity, cost, and value of inventory of direct materials, work in process, finished goods, packing material, spare parts, tools, etc.
    In total
    Separately for each major material, product, etc.
    Identified with each manufacturing division, profit centre, or cost centre
    Comparison of actual quantity and costs with budgeted quantity and costs

Slow moving and obsolete inventory

Inventory variances from the minimum–maximum levels

Purchases of direct materials
    Orders placed, delivery awaited with expected time of delivery
    Purchases of total direct materials, with or without comparison with material purchase budget and analysis of variances
    Purchase price fluctuation report on major direct materials

Reprinted by permission of Publishing Horizons Inc. From *Cost Concepts for Planning, Decisions, and Controls: Concepts and Techniques* by Felix P. Kollaritsch.

Bibliography

Accounting Standards Committee (UK)
SSAP 9, Stocks and Work-in-Progress. The Institute of Chartered Accountants in England and Wales, May 1975

Accounting Standards Committee (UK)
The Corporate Report. The Institute of Chartered Accountants in England and Wales, July 1975

Adelberg, A.
'Resolving Conflicts in Intracompany Transfer Pricing.' *Accountancy*, Volume 98, November 1986, pp. 86–89

Aggarwal, S. C.
'Use of multiple overheads for improving win rate of bids' *Cost and Management* (Canada), July/August 1982, pp. 13–16.

Anthony, R. N. and Dearden, J.
Management Control Systems R. D. Irwin, 1980.

American Accounting Association
'Report of the Committee on Management Accounting.' *Accounting Review*, April 1959, p. 210.

Atkin, B. and Skinner, R.
How British Industry Prices. Industrial Market Research Ltd. 1975

Baxendale, S. J. and Melton, R. N.
'The Internal Audit of Cost Accounting Standards.' *The Internal Auditor* (USA). June 1982, pp. 30–32.

Bourke, P. F.
'What does it cost?' *The Australian Accountant*. April 1969, p. 82.

Belkaoui, A.
Cost Accounting: A Multidimensional Emphasis. CBS College Publishing, 1983.

Benke, R. L. and others.
'Applying an Opportunity Cost General Rule for Transfer Pricing'. *Management Accounting* (USA), June 1982, pp. 43–51.

Binder Hamlyn
: *The Chartac Auditing Manual* Second Edition. Gee & Co., 1986.

Blanchard, G. A. and Chow, C. W.
: 'Allocating Indirect Costs for Improved Management Performance' *Management Accounting* (USA), March 1983, pp. 38–41.

Brimson, J. A.
: 'How Advanced Manufacturing Technologies are Reshaping Cost Management.' *Management Accounting* (USA). March 1986, pp. 25–29.

Cats-Baril, W. L. and others.
: 'Joint Product Costing in the Semiconductor Industry.' *Management Accounting* (USA). February 1986, pp. 28–35.

Challos, P.
: 'High-Tech Production: The Impact on Cost Reporting Systems.' *Journal of Accountancy*, March 1986, pp. 106–112.

Chiu, J. and Lee, Y.
: 'A Survey of Current Practice in Overhead Accounting and Analysis.' Proceedings of the 1980 Western Regional Meeting of the American Accounting Association, O. R. Whittington, Editor, School of Accounting, San Diego State Univ. 1980, p. 242.

Claret, J.
: 'Changing role demands decisions.' *Accountancy Age*. 23 July 1987, p. 24.

Coopers and Lybrand
: *Manual of Auditing* Fourth Edition. Gee and Co., 1984.

Dorward, N.
: 'Overhead Allocations and Optimal Pricing Rules of Thumb in Oligopolistic Markets.' *Accounting and Business Research*. Autumn 1986, pp. 309–317.

Drury, J. C.
: *Management and Cost Accounting*. Van Nostrand Reinhold (UK) Co. Ltd. 1985.

Dudick, T. S.
: *Dudick on Manufacturing Cost Controls*. Prentice-Hall Inc. 1985.

Dudick, T. S.
: 'Why SG & A doesn't always work.' *Harvard Business Review*. January–February 1987, pp. 30–33.

Eccles, R. G.
: *The Transfer Pricing Problem*. D.C. Heath and Company, 1985.

Elphick, C.
: 'Cost Allocation: A New Approach.' *Management Accounting*. December 1985, pp. 22–26.

Financial Accounting Standards Board
: 'Qualitative Characteristics: Criteria for selecting and evaluating Financial Accounting and Reporting Policies.' (Exposure Draft), FASB, 1979.

Fremgen, J. M. and Liao, S.
The Allocation of Corporate Indirect Costs. National Association of Accountants (USA). 1981.

Giacomino, D. E. and Doney, L.D.
'The SAI Movement in Manufacturing.' *The CPA Journal* (USA) No. 10. October 1986, pp. 64–73.

Gilchrist, M. and others.
'Controlling Indirect Costs with Headcount Forecast Algorithms.' *Management Accounting* (USA), August 1985, pp. 46–51.

Govindarjan, V. and Anthony, R. N.
'How Firms Use Cost Data in Price Decisions.' *Management Accounting*. July 1983, pp. 30–36.

Grant Thornton
Audit Manual Third Edition. Longman Group UK Ltd. 1986

Griffiths, I.
Creative Accounting. Waterstone & Co. Ltd. 1986.

Grinnel, D. J. and Mills, J. R.
'Allocating Overhead Costs to Production.' *Managerial Planning* (USA). Mar/Apr 1985. pp. 36–45.

Hill, N. and Dimnik, A.
'The accountant's role in cost-justifying new technologies' *CMA Magazine* (Canada). November–December 1986, pp. 31–37.

Horngren, C. T.
Cost Accounting: A Managerial Emphasis. Fourth Edition. Prentice-Hall Inc., 1977.

Horngren, C. T. and Sorter, G. H.
'Asset Recognition and Economic Attributes – The Relevant Costing Approach.' *The Accounting Review*, July 1962, p. 394.

Hoshower, L. B.
'Appropriate Allocation.' *Management World* (USA). October 1983, pp. 32–36.

Kaplan, R. S.
Advanced Management Accounting. Prentice-Hall. 1982.

Keegan, D. P. and Howard, P. D.
'Transfer Pricing for Fun and Profit.' *Price Waterhouse Review*. Volume 30, No. 3. 1986, pp. 37–45.

Keys, D. E.
'Six Problems in Accounting for N/C Machines.' *Management Accounting* (USA), November 1986, pp. 38–47.

King, A. M.
'Cost Accounting in the 1990s.' *FE: The Magazine for Financial Executives*, November 1986, pp. 24–28.

Kollaritsch, F. P.
   Cost Systems for Planning, Decisions, and Controls: Concepts and Techniques. Grid
   Publishing Inc. 1979.

Krommer, E. L. and Muir, W. T.
   'Measuring Operating Performance through Cost Accounting.' *Price Waterhouse
   Review*, No. 1, 1983, pp. 26–31.

Lawrie, H. R.
   'Full Cost Accounting in the Oil and Gas Industry.' *CA Magazine* (Canada).
   Vol. 119, No. 10. October 1986, pp. 60–62.

Ontario Ministry of Industry
   Trade and Technology; The Market for Flexible Automation Equipment in Ontario,
   1985.

Pyne, F. G.
   'Management accounting in high-technology industries.' *Management Accounting*. July/August 1986, pp. 30–32.

Rahman, M. Z. and Scapens, R. W.
   'Transfer Pricing by Multinationals: Some Evidence from Bangladesh.' *Journal
   of Business Finance & Accounting*. Volume 13, No. 3. Autumn 1986, pp. 383–
   391.

Rayburn, L. G.
   'Principles of Cost Accounting: Managerial Applications.' Third Edition, Irwin
   1986.

Rook, A.
   'Transfer Pricing'. Management Survey Report No. 8. British Institute of Management, 1971.

Rotch, W. et al.
   The Executive's Guide to Management Accounting and Control Systems. Dame
   Publications Inc. 1982.

Seglund, R. and Iberrache, S.
   'Just-in-time: The Accounting Implications.' *Management Accounting* (USA).
   August 1984.

Shah, P. P.
   Cost Control and Information Systems. McGraw Hill, 1981.

Sizer, J.
   'Pricing Policy in inflation: A management accountant's perspective.' *Accounting
   and Business Research*. Spring 1976, pp. 107–124.

Skinner, R. C.
   'The Determination of Selling Prices.' *Journal of Industrial Economics*. July 1970,
   pp. 201–217.

Spicer and Pegler
   Practical Auditing Seventh Edition. Butterworth. 1985.

Swann, D. M.
'Where Did the Inventory Go?' *Management Accounting* (USA). May 1986, pp. 27–29.

Thomson McLintock & Co.
The Thomson McLintock Audit Manual. Macmillan, 1983.

Tomkins, C.
Financial Planning in Divisionalized Companies. Haymarket Publishing Company, 1973.

Woodward, A.
'Causal Costing: Why, not where.' *Management Accounting.* May 1986, pp. 24–25.

Wright, H. W.
'Uniform Cost Accounting Standards: Past, Present, and Future.' *Financial Executive* (USA), May 1971.

Zimmerman, J. L.
'The Costs and Benefits of Cost Allocations.' *The Accounting Review.* July 1979, pp. 504–521.

Journal articles

(In order of appearance)
Chadwick L. 'The Costs of Holding Stocks.'
Management Services.   October 1982
Aspinall D. and Chadwick L. 'The Sub Contracting Decision.'
Management Accounting.   June 1985
Bethune H. and Chadwick L. 'The Case of the Half-A-Million Pounds Stock Deficit.'
Retail and Distribution Management.   May/June 1983
Chadwick L. 'Absorption Costing – a critical view.'
Certified Accountants' Students' Newsletter.   December 1987
Chadwick L. 'Service Department Costs – a critical view.'
Certified Accountants' Students' Newsletter.   January 1988
Chadwick L. 'Marginal Costing – a critical view.'
Certified Accountants' Students' Newsletter.   February 1988
Chadwick L. 'Process Costing – a critical view.'
Certified Accountants' Students' Newsletter.   March 1988
Chadwick L. 'Capital Investment Appraisal – which discount rate?'
Certified Accountants' Students' Newsletter.   March 1987
Chadwick L. 'Capital Investment Appraisal and The Tax Factor.'
Certified Accountants' Students' Newsletter.   December 1986
Chadwick L. 'Money Doesn't Mean Everything: The Non-Financial Aspects of Capital Investment Appraisal.'
Accountants Weekly   12 June 1981

Chadwick L. and Rogers D. 'How to Cost the Right Price.'
The Accountant. 11 October 1984
Chadwick L. and Rogers D. 'Making the Price Decision.'
The Accountant. 8 November 1984

We would like to thank all of the copyright holders for permission to reproduce the above-mentioned journal articles.

INDEX